HOW TO STUDY M

How to Study
Series editors: John Peck and Martin Coyle

IN THE SAME SERIES

HOW TO STUDY
MODERN DRAMA

Kenneth Pickering

MACMILLAN

First published 1988 by
THE MACMILLAN PRESS LTD
Houndmills, Basingstoke, Hampshire RG21 2XS
and London
Companies and representatives
throughout the world

ISBN 0–333–42864–1

A catalogue record for this book is available
from the British Library.

12 11 10 9 8 7 6 5
03 02 01 00 99 98 97 96

Printed in Hong Kong

Contents

General editors' preface

EVERYBODY who studies literature, either for an examination or simply for pleasure, experiences the same problem: how to understand and respond to the text. As every student of literature knows, it is perfectly possible to read a book over and over again and yet still feel baffled and at a loss as to what to say about it. One answer to this problem, of course, is to accept someone else's view of the text, but how much more rewarding it would be if you could work out your own critical response to any book you choose or are required to study.

The aim of this series is to help you develop your critical skills by offering practical advice about how to read, understand and analyse literature. Each volume provides you with a clear method of study so that you can see how to set about tackling texts on your own. While the authors of each volume approach the problem in a different way, every book in the series attempts to provide you with some broad ideas about the kind of texts you are likely to be studying and some broad ideas about how to think about literature; each volume then shows you how to apply these ideas in a way which should help you construct your own analysis and interpretation. Unlike most critical books, therefore, the books in this series do not simply convey someone else's thinking about a text, but encourage you and show you how to think about a text for yourself.

Each book is written with an awareness that you are likely to be preparing for an examination, and therefore practical advice is given not only on how to understand and analyse literature, but also on how to organise a written response. Our hope is that although these books are intended to serve a practical purpose, they may also enrich your enjoyment of literature by making you a more confident reader, alert to the interest and pleasure to be derived from literary texts.

John Peck
Martin Coyle

Acknowledgements

THE author wishes to express grateful thanks to Kevin Wood and the cast of Channel Theatre's production of *The Birthday Party* for many new insights; to Jean and Irene Pickering for their careful work on the manuscript; and to Martin Coyle and John Peck for their seemingly inexhaustible supply of helpful suggestions.

The author and publishers gratefully acknowledge permission to use copyright material granted by the following:

Professor Shelley Frome and the editor of *Speech and Drama*; Jonathan Cape Ltd for extracts from the works of Wesker; Eyre Methuen Ltd for extracts from plays by Harold Pinter, Shelagh Delaney, Bertold Brecht and Henrik Ibsen; Faber and Faber for an extract from *Look Back in Anger*; Penguin Plays for extracts from *Death of a Salesman*.

For Susannah and Simon

1

Introduction

How to use this book

THE aim of this book is to enable you to make a really good job of responding to any modern play that you might encounter as part of a course at school, college or university. Students are often very worried about studying modern plays, either because they are completely baffled as to what a play is about or because they have read or seen a particular play, enjoyed it, but simply cannot think what else to say about it when it comes to analysis. In either case the prospect of writing an essay or examination answer seems daunting.

I should not be writing this book to help you if I did not feel certain that studying modern plays *can* and *should* be one of the most fascinating and enjoyable experiences in the whole field of literature and drama, but I have to admit that there are two particular reasons why it might not appear to be so. Firstly, there are some modern plays which seem utterly incomprehensible when you initially encounter them, and you should never be ashamed to confess that this is the case. Don't be depressed: plenty of sophisticated audiences and critics have at first been totally perplexed by plays that have later established themselves as classics, and one of the many options open to a playwright *is* to mystify the audience. Secondly, we are all now bombarded with drama through television, so that we are likely to consume more modern drama than novels, poetry or earlier drama. Because we watch so many soap operas, domestic comedies, documentary dramas, one-off plays and so on, it is difficult to conceive of 'studying' an art form we take so much for granted.

How, then, *do* we study a modern play, and how can this book help? Almost certainly you will have acquired this book because you are about to be or already have been set the task of studying a particular play and so are looking for practical guidance on how to come to grips with it. Initially I am going to ask you to consider three questions of a general nature before going on to suggest a number of steps to follow in studying a modern play. The discussion of those three questions will occupy the remainder of this chapter, and if you take the time and trouble to make sure that you have grasped the issues, the rest of the task will be much simpler and *much* more interesting.

After looking at our three questions I shall then go on to suggest a number of steps to take in the study of modern plays. You need to master each stage before going onto the next and so, clearly, we cannot consider all the steps at once. Each step will be applied to examples from well-known plays, but once you have worked through the examples provided you should try the idea out on one of your own set plays. Later in the book we shall be considering other possible ways of approaching play study, and then all the techniques discussed will be brought together to demonstrate how you should tackle an extract, essay or examination question.

As you acquire new skills and insights you should find yourself able to go deeper into a play and growing in confidence as you discover that you are able to make valuable judgements about the material. In particular I am anxious that you will come to 'make sense' of what is really a strange and remarkable ritual: a group of people, with you amongst them, sits in a darkened room and watch another group of people perform in an agreed space. The first group of people, the *audience*, never invades the space of the second group of people, the *cast*, nor do they normally shout out when they are angry, bored or mystified. Indeed, the audience allows the cast to insult them, shock them, amuse them and manipulate their perception in a whole variety of ways. The audience, for example, may agree to imagine that a structure on the stage is a room in someone's house or that a bare stage represents the universe, or that half an hour represents several hours. The cast may speak directly to the audience or appear to pretend that the audience does not exist. This ritual we call 'theatre' is stranger the more you think about it, and modern plays are the product of what playwrights have felt to be appropriate forms of this ritual in recent years. And this leads to our first question.

What is a 'modern' play?

The precise meaning of the term 'modern' varies according to its context. If I were to drive a 1930s car or to wear clothes that were fashionable only ten years ago you certainly wouldn't describe my tastes as modern; yet we usually describe as modern any play written since 1877! In this particular year the great Norwegian dramatist Ibsen turned from writing plays in verse to create a series of plays in everyday language dealing with important social and moral issues. It was the impact of these and similar plays on the European theatre of the late nineteenth century and the rapid spread of their influence to Britain, Russia and the United States of America that began the era of 'modern drama'.

The style of Ibsen's plays is frequently labelled 'naturalistic', and while there have been many departures from naturalism in the modern age it has remained the dominant mode and, for most of us, the most accessible form of theatre. Television has only strengthened the hold of naturalism. Though we shall return to the idea many times, it is important to note here that we generally *expect* a play to be naturalistic; that is, to show us believable people living credible lives and speaking like ourselves. Because naturalistic plays are the most straightforward to deal with, my early examples will be drawn from this kind of play.

Before we leave the question of what is meant by 'modern drama', you must surely be asking whether the fact that certain plays were written after a certain date is sufficient reason for lumping them all together under one heading. Clearly they must have a few other things in common, and three factors are particularly helpful to consider.

First, modern plays all in some way concern the predicament of man living in the age of science and industrialisation. This is a bold statement, and when you have read this book and studied your plays you may wish to challenge it, but you will find that even modern plays which are *set* in earlier periods of history are still inviting the judgements of modern, scientific man.

Secondly, modern plays in some way reflect the remarkable changes in theatre design and technology which occurred towards the end of the nineteenth century and have continued ever since. Theatres have, of course, always been subject to change, but the rapidity of change in the last hundred years has been unprecedented: it is a period which has seen the invention of the electric light and has now reached a point where through television we can each have our own theatre. Shapes of stages and theatre buildings have been subject to constant experiment, so that playwrights are constantly challenged to rethink their craft. Audiences have also been experimented upon; for example, it is only during the period of modern drama that they have sat in a darkened auditorium. So you must remember that any modern play you are studying was written for a sophisticated yet frequently changing theatre.

Thirdly, you will find that, in comparison with the plays of Shakespeare, modern plays are very much more varied in form. They include some extremely long plays, such as Shaw's *Man and Superman*, but also many short ones, such as the one-act plays by Pinter and the thirty-second play *Breath* by Beckett. To some extent the prevalence of short plays reflects tastes and habits: the pace of modern life generally seems to call for shorter plays; but it also stems from the development of many non-commercial and experimental theatres which may have small numbers of performers but also a greater freedom to try out new ideas. Among modern plays, however, you will find many that conform to the structure of three acts with one or two scenes, a structure often used by Ibsen and his successors; unlike Shakespeare's plays they present a series of episodes of roughly equal length each with its own climax. Studying a modern play includes discovering how its particular structure works, and we need to avoid any idea that there is a 'right' way for a playwright to structure his work.

What is a playtext?

When you are studying any form of drama you must be constantly aware that a 'play' really only exists when it is performed. A playtext, on which most study is centred, is only the complex set of instructions to the performers. Because the bulk of a playtext consists of the words which the cast must speak, and because words are chosen or shaped with great skill, the playtext itself is often mistakenly thought to be simply another literary form like the novel or poetry. Small wonder that some students find plays difficult to understand, since they have not grasped that the 'meaning' of a play only emerges in the theatre.

The implication of this is that in studying a play you must recognise that the words spoken by the characters are only one element, and I shall be suggesting ways in which you can interpret the various other indications for performance contained in a playtext. Furthermore, as you study a play you will need to construct an imaginary performance in your mind. This may well cause you problems because you may have such limited experience of the theatre; again there are suggested activities in this book which will help you overcome this factor. Obviously you will need to see the play you are studying performed as often as possible, but this may not be easy and you may well experience a sharp clash between the imaginary performance you have created in your mind and a live performance you may see. None of these problems, however, are insurmountable, and indeed you will find the exploration of various interpretations of a play very stimulating. You can imagine how dull it would be if all performances of a particular piece of music were identical, but, similarly, how absurd it would be to study music without imagining it being played or sung.

In the modern theatre the majority of successful playwrights have been deeply involved in the performance of their plays and, as I have already indicated, this has been a period of rapid change and bold experimentation. Playwrights have conveyed many of their wishes and attitudes concerning the performance of their plays in the published playtexts, so when you begin reading the play (which can be a very enjoyable activity in its own right) remember you are not studying a novel.

What is 'study' in relation to modern drama?

The most likely reason for your having obtained this book is that you are a full-time student required to study plays, but you are not the only kind of person who 'studies' plays, and plays were not written to be set for examination purposes. You may dismiss this last remark as trivial and hardly worth your serious consideration, but it does have serious implications. If plays were written for performance, then it follows that those who have to be involved in performing them – actors, directors, designers – need to study them with as much perception, care and imagination as students. Such people must ask the same crucial question as students of every playtext they encounter: 'How are the playwright's intentions realised in performance?'

Students can learn much from the way in which actors and directors approach the study of a play and you will benefit from tackling a play *as if* the end product were a production rather than an essay. Some of the suggestions in this book might provide insights into ways of doing this. The idea of 'study' is usually associated with reading, solitary contemplation and quiet reflection, all of which is valuable. But in the case of drama there are other dimensions. 'Study' may involve theatre visits, play-reading and other practical ways of exploring a text. There is not a division between activity and thinking: on the contrary, there is clearly established link between thought and action, so do not be surprised if you only come to understand a line when you have to speak it for yourself or if you only realise the impact of an entrance of a character into a room when you have experienced it in performance.

Do not be alarmed by the idea of performance. The aim of this book is not to make an actor or actress of you and there *will* be a strong emphasis on traditional, bookish study. However, the *possibility* of performance must always be in your mind and there are various practical activities that are helpful without demanding a high level of acting-skill. There is, though, no substitute for quietly reading the play – so this is where we shall begin.

2

First reading

LET us suppose that you are required to study Arthur Miller's play *Death of a Salesman*, written in 1948. You may know nothing about the playwright except, perhaps, that he was once married to Marilyn Monroe and that in terms of dates he fits the label 'modern dramatist'. Initially you should aim to read through the entire play as quickly and comfortably as possible. No modern play is likely to take more than a few hours to read and you should get used to the idea of reading it several times at varying levels. Your *first* reading is almost certainly going to be more like reading a novel; you will probably picture the events taking place in real life rather than on a stage, and your response will be emotional, focused on the characters and their situations, rather than the critical, analytic response which we are finally hoping to achieve. Inevitably at this stage you will find yourself skimming over the lengthy stage directions and giving most attention to what the characters say. In *Death of a Salesman*, however, you will discover that you cannot afford to disregard the stage directions entirely or you will become utterly confused, especially by the sections which use a 'flashback' technique; but for the time being some of the precise instructions embedded in the stage directions can be set aside. The fact that I need to mention this at all does, though, highlight another characteristic of modern drama: this is that the material contained in a playtext is a great deal more than dialogue, especially when compared with a Shakespeare play.

As a result of your first, rapid reading you should be able to identify a number of *important features* upon which you will be able to build your critical response. If you do not bear these in mind, your reading will be aimless and probably of little value; more important, these features will help you to make sense of your first contact with the play.

Action

The first general aspect of the play that you should be able to discuss after an initial reading is what actually *happens*. Be careful here, though. Students often place far too much emphasis on this element and so offer a summary of the story-line or plot as a substitute for a critical commentary. One reason for this is that they fail to distinguish between the play's *story*, its *action* and its *performance*. A play tells the story and the outline of that story must be clear in your mind by the time you finish reading the play. So, for example, we can say that Miller's *Death of a Salesman* tells the story of a salesman, Willy Loman, and how his life slowly disintegrates into failure until he kills himself.

This story, however, is not told in a straightforward chronological sequence; instead, events from the past are interspersed among scenes from the present. Strictly speaking, the story begins in the scenes set furthest in the past, but the action of the play begins in the present. What the *action* of the play does is to show and explain the death of Willy Loman by a deliberate juxtaposing of scenes and effects. As you read a play, you should be aware of this distinction between story and action: think of the action of the play as *the way* in which the story is presented and organised so as to bring out its meaning. *Death of a Salesman*, for example, clearly tells the story of Willy Loman's life and death; the action of the play, however, shows us how Willy is a victim of the American Dream of modern society and its values.

One complication that you need to be aware of is that the action of a play really embraces *all* that occurs during a *performance* of a play. A performance of a play is obviously impossible to reproduce just by reading it, but what you can seize upon to help you grasp the full action of the play is the *activity* in a theatrical performance. The actors playing the characters in *Death of a Salesman* are given dozens of activities by the playwright. They drink, get out of bed, move in specified ways, smoke, laugh, and so on. Modern plays are dense with such instructions and clearly you cannot hope to retain all these details even after several readings. This does not make them unimportant; on the contrary, playwrights since Ibsen have found it essential to provide minute details of the activities of the characters in their plays so as to convey a full sense of them as human beings caught in a particular world, and we can never hope to grasp the meaning of a play without considering these issues. However, this is a matter for detailed scene study rather than general reading, and it is quite sufficient if, on your first contact with the play, you use these activities to lend your reading imaginative life. If you can also remember one or two details of such activities – for example, in *Death of a Salesman* we constantly see characters going to the refrigerator, or sitting down at the family table alone – that would be a bonus, for it will help you discipline your thinking by having something concrete to build on.

The protagonist's predicament

So far in our initial reading of the play we have been concerned not with *how* the dramatist conveys ideas or impressions, but simply with the material itself. The same applies at this stage to our next consideration – the protagonist's (central character's) predicament. Plays inevitably show characters in struggle against some problem or series of problems which threaten to overwhelm them. In modern drama the *protagonist* or *hero* possess so few of the heroic qualities we traditionally associate with that title that he is often known as an *anti-hero*, while the problems with which he is confronted are often domestic rather than of the grandiose, cosmic scale of Shakespeare. At a personal level, however, the outcome may be equally tragic, disturbing or harrowing.

By the conclusion of your first reading and consideration of the play you should be able to summarise both the action of the play and the central predicament in which the protagonist finds himself. The effect on you as a reader will be cumulative, because as you progress through the play further complications of the predicament will emerge. It is a good idea to note them down as you go.

Willy Loman's main predicament in *Death of a Salesman* is that he is in a situation to which he is entirely unfitted: he must live and support his family by being a salesman, yet his personality militates against success; he lives in an enclosed space, yet his nature longs for wide open spaces. He has added to his predicament by a number of fatal errors of judgement: his brief unfaithfulness to his wife has permanently poisoned his relationship with his favourite son; the attitudes he has encouraged in Biff have contributed to the latter's failure at school in 'math'. In order to cope with the increasing pressures, Willy has manufactured a network of lies in which he has become trapped. So Willy is trapped in three ways: by his job, by his house and by his own deceit – inevitably there is only one ultimate means of escape.

Arthur Miller has chosen a particularly effective means by which to establish Willy Loman's predicament in theatrical terms, and the résumé I have offered only suggests the level of awareness you might reasonably be expected to reach after a single, rapid reading of the play. The issue is by no means exhausted, but if you pay attention to both the action of the play and also to the predicament of the main character, you should be able to say in general terms what the play you are studying is about.

Tensions and threats

Much of the fascination of plays stems from the interaction between the different characters. This aspect of a play only emerges fully in performance, but even at the early reading stage it is possible and essential to identify the sources of tension. The protagonist's predicament often engulfs and is frequently derived from other characters, yet we must not neglect to notice the tensions between lesser characters as well. *Identifying the lines of tension* between characters is another function of a first reading and again it is something you should note down as you read.

Interest in the way that people relate to each other is a particular feature of modern drama. It is partly a result of the developing science of psychology, which was in its infancy when Ibsen wrote his first naturalistic play. Modern playwrights are operating in a world which generally attempts to explain people's behaviour in rational, scientific terms and which sees individuals as needing to succeed in personal relationships in order to achieve a sense of well-being and social adjustment. Social order and personal happiness are threatened by tensions between individuals or groups; tensions force us into playing different roles, adapting our behaviour to suit a situation; tensions may become obsessive fears.

If there were no tensions in a play or in life there would be perfect harmony but little interest. In drama, as in life, we look for a resolution of tensions and that is what makes characters in plays struggle on. The tramps in Beckett's *Waiting for Godot* (1953), for example, endure a restless state of waiting because there is the hope that when Godot comes there will be some kind of resolution. Davies, the old tramp in Harold Pinter's *The Caretaker* (1960), struggles to find a way of resolving the tension that has developed between himself and his new landlord Aston.

The major sources of tension in a play should therefore be one of your first concerns. The first few pages of *Death of a Salesman* show how relatively easy the tensions are to spot. As Willy replies to Linda's first questions about his day, there is already a hint of irritation and reluctance to give a straight answer. When Willy does explain his utter exhaustion, there is an element of refusal to face the facts in Linda's reply. Soon we hear of tension between Willy and his employers, a frightening tension between Willy and his son Biff, and also of conflicting perceptions of each other by father and son. Characters and situations also pose *threats* to other characters. We feel that Willy Loman sees Charley, his neighbour, as a threat to his self-esteem; Bernard, one of Biff's contemporaries and rivals, threatens to expose the false values Willy has instilled into his son; and, above all, the *past* threatens every aspect of Willy's present life. The past means that Willy must always delude himself and others, and this creates constant tension.

In your critical response to a play you are going to have to evaluate the dramatist's methods of showing the tensions and threats which govern the behaviour of the characters he has created. During and *just after* your first reading you will be concentrating on what characters say and do in the context of their developing situations, and you should ensure that you have a clear idea of the main features of the relationships between characters. You may need to go back over the play very quickly to check details and impressions and you *may* find it helpful to draw a diagram consisting of circles for each character and arrows joining them indicating possible causes of tension. You may have to ask such questions as 'Does she suspect him?' or 'Did one event in the past affect this relationship?' So many modern plays examine the effect of the past on the present that this second question is almost inevitable.

Identifying the 'world' of the play and its social order

In addition to having some clear idea about the kinds of tension there are in the play you are studying, you should come from your first reading of a play with a clear idea of the kind of world that it is about. For the purposes of a play the writer creates an entire fictional world in which to set the action. That world may be unfamiliar to us, as in Arthur Miller's *The Crucible*, or remarkably familiar to us, as in *Death of a Salesman*, but as readers and audience we must believe in its reality and grasp its characteristics and pressures.

The world of *Death of a Salesman* is the modern consumer society: a world in which people buy goods with built-in obsolescence on credit and struggle to pay off mortgages for the duration of their lives. Technology produces new gadgets which the wealthy use for pleasure and the not-so-wealthy feel pressurised into buying. The other half of that world consists of the salesmen themselves, dedicated to enticing people to spend, driving thousands of miles, their success depending on the precarious business of getting people to part with their money, the gap between success and failure perilously narrow. The salesmen must cultivate 'push', 'drive' and ruthlessness. This is a society which can treat its individuals like its goods – they can be thrown away once they are worn out – but during their useful lives they can be kept in boxes. The pressures on individuals and families in such a situation are immense and inevitably parents hope for better things for their children.

If we are entirely honest, nothing about the world of *Death of a Salesman* should come as a surprise: newspapers are still full of advertisements for salespeople who will recklessly drive their cars and themselves in the hope of rich rewards, but the promise of high earnings for the successful are phoney; we continue to house vast sections of our populations in conditions which exclude the possibility of a garden or even sunlight; true, the latest electronic 'necessity' may not be the tape-recorder, as it is in the play, but its contemporary equivalent is all too obvious. So, in some respects, the setting of *Death of a Salesman* in the late 1940s is almost irrelevant provided we understand the *kind* of world the play establishes.

All that I have discussed so far can easily be established from a first reading of the play, but it is also important that you link it to the *social order* presented and subsequently threatened by the events of the play. Man attempts to live in a society by creating a sense of order, and in a play it is quite easy to identify this ideal state to which a particular society is striving. In *Death of a Salesman*, for example, it is clear that the family is seen as the basis of society, and also as an ideal of social order. From the very start of the play tenderness and concern are expressed by wife for husband, father feels love and anxiety for his sons; home is the base to which they all come and in which the mother has a caring role. The disappointment in Biff which Willy endures seems a product of a father's legitimate pride and aspirations; the pressure on Willy partially stems from his having to provide for his family. The fact that we soon discover that this sense of order is threatened because it is based on illusions and delusions makes it all the more important to grasp.

Think, also, of the wider social order of adulthood and work. Happy and Biff, Willy's sons, 'should' be married, with families and careers of their own. Having a career ought to provide challenge and fulfilment; workers should be respected, long and valued service to a company ought to be recognised; a man should be able to own a house, a car and a refrigerator without a sense of constant burden. In personal relations there should be sensitivity, gratitude, an appreciation of personal dignity.

These are the features of the social order which the characters in *Death of a Salesman* are trying to build. It is obvious from a very early stage that it will crumble, and part of the fascination in the first reading is to see how and to what extent it does. You should always try to summarise briefly the world of the play you are studying and the particular features of the social order that under-pin all the play's action. Some plays will provide a much narrower or wider perspective than *Death of a Salesman*: Beckett's *Waiting for Godot*, for example, concentrates entirely upon two tramps who remain by a roadside throughout the play and who have established their own social order, a social order which hardly relates to the rest of the world and which is threatened by the two appearances of Lucky and Pozzo and the non-appearance of a mysterious Mr Godot; in contrast again, Miller's *The Crucible* presents a complex society structured around the authority of families and employers in relation to the ultimate authority of the church. A few sentences describing your understanding of these essential features of a play will provide you with an overall grasp of the larger significance of the play you are studying and how it is about much broader issues than just the experiences of this or that character, how it deals with the large questions of man's place in the social order.

Conducting your initial analysis: a step-by-step guide, with example

By this stage you may be feeling overwhelmed by all that you are expected to achieve in a single reading. There is no need to panic: we all have our own comfortable rate of absorption, and, if it takes you two or more readings to complete to your satisfaction, what has been set out here then that is perfectly reasonable. The important fact to grasp, however, is that, whatever line your study of a play will eventually take or whatever question you are trying to answer, there is no point in going on to more specific or detailed study until you have mastered the material by using the steps suggested here:

1 *Achieve a broad outline of the action*
2 *Define the protagonist's predicament*
3 *Trace the main tensions and threats in the play*
4 *Examine the world of the play and its social order*

In order to illustrate how these basic steps can be used to approach a modern play, and how to draw things together, it might be helpful if I provide a further brief example here before we move on to the next stage in Chapter 3. The play I have chosen to concentrate on here is **The Caretaker** (1960), by Harold Pinter.

1   *Achieve a broad outline of the action*

In certain respects not a great deal actually 'happens' in *The Caretaker*; although the playwright has provided a great deal of *activity* for the actors, there are relatively few major incidents. Much of the play's action is taken up with talk in which the characters generally fail to communicate with each other. This failure is a key to the real action of the play, which remains taut and compelling throughout.

The action of the play is set in a single junk-filled room and occupies four days plus a further two days a fortnight later. After a mysterious opening in which a man, who turns out to be Mick, sits on a bed looking up at a bucket into which water is dripping and then leaves the stage, Aston (Mick's brother) brings in Davies, a tramp who he has rescued from a café brawl. The shy Aston treats Davies kindly and asks him if he would like to be caretaker. Davies, who shows himself to be entirely self-regarding and who brags pathetically, grudgingly accepts. Davies' past and even his identity are doubtful, but Aston continues to treat him with kindness and reveals a great deal about himself in a long, monologue-like speech. Meanwhile, Mick has been observing Davies and alternatively scares him and leads him on with the offer of the job of caretaker. Davies, thinking he has gained Mick's confidence, becomes openly aggressive to Aston and eventually threatens and taunts him with references to his mental illness. Aston, with an immense effort, suggests that Davies should leave and when Davies turns to Mick for support he finds himself abruptly dismissed from his 'caretaking'. Desperately Davies now turns back to Aston, suggesting that he take over Aston's bed; but this is a final encroachment and the play ends with Aston turning away.

If you have read *The Caretaker* you will know that this summary of the play's action does not give any hint of some of its more disturbing activities, such as the incident when Aston and Mick throw Davies's bag around the stage in a bizarre teasing game. It will often be the case that you notice such puzzling things in modern plays, but don't let this deter you from achieving a clear sense of the play's overall action; don't allow the details of the play to prevent you from getting hold of its basic action.

2   *Define the protagonist's predicament*

The first tricky question is 'Who *is* the protagonist?' In terms of interest and the number of lines they speak, the characters of Aston and Davies seem about equal. Is this, then, a play like *Waiting for Godot*, where there are clearly *two* protagonists? You might wish to argue differently, but the fact that *every* scene shows one or both of the brothers relating to the tramp Davies, who is on stage for all but the opening minute of the play, suggests that Davies is the central character. Pinter reinforces this by naming the play *The Caretaker*, the role which Davies is supposed to fill.

Davies is used to sleeping rough; he is defensive, absurdly prejudiced, vague about the past, apparently threatened by almost everybody with whom he comes into contact. He is a social outcast with no roots, no hope, no social competence. His world is governed by where he will scrounge his next cup of tea or pair of shoes. Suddenly he is offered the chance of a permanent base, but he cannot understand the environment into which he has been brought, nor the two people who inhabit or visit it. Desperately he has to try to readjust to their conduct and at the same time to contend with his own contradictory rag-bag of attitudes. The longer Davies stays, the more comfortable he becomes in the physical sense, but the more futile are his efforts to break into the tight framework which exists before he came; he simply cannot respond adequately to the demands of the situation.

3   *Trace the main tensions and threats in the play*

There are only three characters in this play, and at certain points there is tension between all of them. Possible tension is suggested at the very beginning when Mick leaves the stage *before* Aston enters with Davies – there is clearly a strange relationship between the two brothers. Davies seems ill at ease but is gradually relaxed by Aston's kindness. However, Davies then questions the nature of the room – who is outside, who shares the bathroom, the broken window, the junk, the gas-stove. Such criticism is unacceptable to Aston; it seems ungrateful. Davies' snorings and gibberings in the night, and later his smell, upset Aston and deprive him of sleep. The tramp's response is aggressive and he views Aston with increasing incomprehension.

The tension between Mick and Davies is manipulated by the former and leaves the latter wriggling like a fish on a hook. In the famous scene where Davies' bag and trousers are passed back and forth, Aston has to intervene out of character to break the pattern. Twice Mick terrifies and intimidates Davies, and the tramp acts in the continual aftermath of these incidents. When, however, Davies thinks he has detected a way to undermine Aston by exploiting any possible gulf between the brothers, Mick closes the gap, violently. We suspect that, in a strange way, Mick may be afraid of Aston.

All the characters in *The Caretaker* feel threatened: Aston by the world outside and by the intrusion of Davies when he seeks to upset the social order; Davies, by authority, bureaucracy, the past, questions and by anything or anybody he doesn't understand; Mick, by Aston's introduction of Davies. Mick uses violence and language to threaten Davies; an obscure sense of threat from the outside broods over the entire play.

4   *Examine the world of the play and its social order*

The Caretaker deals with people who live in the run-down, seedy environment of a present-day city suburb. Large houses that were once rather 'smart' are now divided into flats, and people of various races live in the dingy accommodation provided. It is an area of small cafés, junk-shops and pubs; there is little sense of community in the broad meaning of that word; there is suspicion and prejudice between racial groups. We would term the environment as one of some 'social deprivation'. Yet this is a world in which some *own* property and a relatively small minority make decisions which affect the lives of others. It is a fundamentally materialistic society and there are some who 'drop out' from the rat race and come to be regarded as 'odd'. A particularly potent example of this is the treatment of mental illness, which has become impersonal and brutal, no adequate provision being made for rehabilitation of patients into society.

Mick has been relatively successful: he is a quick thinker,

smooth talker and he feels at ease in the world. He has acquired a property in some stage of dilapidation and allowed his brother, Aston, to live in part of it. Aston is mild and incompetent, slow to make decisions and unable to act upon them. He makes few demands of life and lives surrounded by various objects he has accumulated, dreaming only of the shed he will one day build in the garden. The arrangement between Mick, who is obviously concerned for his brother, and Aston, who is a 'drop out', clearly suits them both. Although to outside eyes the room in which he lives, cluttered with useless junk, may seem absurd, to Aston it represents familiarity, security and a refuge. When a new character, Davies – a tramp on whom Aston has taken pity – enters the room, the whole social order is threatened.

As with my remarks on *Death of a Salesman*, you might feel that you could not sum up your impressions of the play you are studying in the way I have after just a single reading. Once again the advice is to take your time and establish a firm grasp of the four features I have described. What will help you do this is if you can see how both *Death of a Salesman* and *The Caretaker* are built around a common pattern, a common tension between, on the one hand, the idea of social order, and, on the other, the idea of disorder, threats, tensions which undermine that order. If you keep this pattern in mind, it will help you clarify all the four features I have described, as it will also help you move forward in your study of the play as a play, as something seen and acted. In other words you will start to come to grips with the play as a piece of drama rather than as a story with speaking characters.

If you are fortunate enough to begin your study of a play by seeing it performed in a theatre you should be able to use the four steps I have described as a means of making sense of the experience. The impact of a live performance is obviously different from a reading, because in the theatre you are responding to a succession of images carefully shaped by the playwright and director. Your reading *must* take account of what happens in performance if you are to do full justice to the play, and in order to do this you need to understand some of the *conventions* of theatre. We can make this into another step:

5   *Think about the play in performance*

The basic conventions of the theatre are very easy to understand and will add a great deal to your enjoyment in studying a play. After you have finished reading your play, look back over it and consider the following three factors: language; setting; and plot, action and activity.

(a) *Language*. The playwright has provided the words for the actors to speak and these words represent 'real' speech. In the majority of modern plays the similarity between the language of plays and that of ordinary people in everyday life is considerable. The two plays we have considered are particularly good examples. In the theatre we usually accept that the words being spoken are appropriate to the people talking, although at times playwrights manipulate us into accepting that a very specialised kind of theatre language is 'real' dialogue between people. I have never heard anyone at a performance of T. S. Eliot's *Murder in the Cathedral* complain that 'people don't talk like that', even though the play is written in verse; there is, as it were, an unspoken contract between actors and audience that, for the duration of the play, that is how the characters will converse.

All stage dialogue, however natural it may seem, is highly selective and artificial. Studying a play involves an examination of the style, form and content of the language and at this stage you should notice its general characteristics. Notice, for example, which characters do the *most* speaking; note any particularly *long* speeches and *to whom* characters address themselves. Some modern playwrights give their characters speeches addressed directly at the audience; other characters appear to speak mainly to themselves; while other plays yet again give the *impression* of normal conversation.

The two plays we have considered provide excellent examples of the way in which the language works through the conventions of performance. Aston's huge speech which concludes Act II of *The Caretaker* – probably the longest speech you will encounter in any play – seems quite unacceptable on the page. Quite apart from its rather slow and tedious progress it seems incredible that anyone would really talk for that long. Yet, in the theatre, this speech, delivered in the narrowing circle of a single spotlight with the baffled Davies looking on, is a gripping experience, invariably felt in intense silence by the audience.

In *Death of a Salesman* we accept without difficulty that Happy and Biff are talking in their bedroom but that we can also hear Willy's words from the living-room. At times we also receive a particular impression from the juxtaposition of the words of the play with the sound of a flute. In the same way a play may include moments when we, the audience, hear what a character on stage is saying but the other characters on stage do not. Such aspects of a play will only have meaning in performance, but as a student you must cultivate the habit of noticing and *imaginatively reconstructing* them in the process of reading the play.

(b) *Setting*. There is nothing modern about the idea that a stage can represent any place that a dramatist chooses. From your study of Shakespeare you will probably be familiar with the convention of a bare stage being transformed into a whole range of locations in the imaginations of the audience simply by the language of the performers. In the modern period, however, advances in theatre technology have enabled playwrights to demand real transformation of stage spaces so that they either closely resemble the environment they are supposed to represent or create a striking visual image of an expressionist or symbolic nature. Stage design has become a highly specialised aspect of theatre arts which the playwright cannot ignore. Some modern playwrights have exploited the fairly recent rediscovery of the power of the stage as a relatively empty space and have deliberately set their plays at odds with the expectation of audiences for naturalistic settings.

The environment in which the characters of a drama exist is an important entity in the modern theatre. From your reading of the play you must begin to imagine that environment and the way in which characters interact with it. Many modern plays, such as *The Caretaker*, are set in a single room. This alone is a significant fact and tells us a good deal about the preoccupations of modern writers. Playwrights such as Ibsen, Shaw and Pinter give us quite specific instructions concerning the room. In most cases they presuppose a stage setting in which the room is constructed on stage and the audience watches through the gap where the 'fourth wall' would normally be. In such a situation the actors behave as if the fourth wall were actually there; indeed, one modern director, Antoine, went to the trouble of constructing a fourth wall during rehearsals, to ensure that his cast acted in that way. However, because we as audience expect both to see and to hear all the performance, the actors make certain modifications to their behaviour to make this possible. Were a modern play set in a single room to be presented 'in-the-round', with the audience sitting on all four sides, the director would have to ensure that the room without walls contained sufficient features representative of the playwright's intentions to create the same powerful image.

In *The Caretaker* it is the junk cluttering Aston's room which is so important. It is not just that a performance would be less effective without it; the whole meaning of the playing depends on seeing Aston in this environment. Objects such as the bucket hanging from the ceiling, the gas stove, the window or the Buddha are as much a part of the play as the 'language' or the 'characters', with which students tend to become preoccupied. *Death of a Salesman* works through another convention – the *multiple setting*. Here the playwright enables us to witness several rooms in a house simultaneously. Consider how revealing this would be were we able to do this in real life! This play owes much of its power to the simple convention of making this possible. The same flexibility enables Arthur Miller to move backwards and forwards in time – a feature with which Pinter has experimented in recent plays – and, again, the audience accepts these conventions.

Perhaps the most significant demand Miller makes at the very beginning of *Death of a Salesman* is in the stage directions: '*We are aware of towering, angular shapes behind it, surrounding it on all sides.*' I readily admit that, were I simply to have read that on the first page of the play I should probably have forgotten it by the second. But it is Miller's intention that we should never forget it, and in the theatre we must never be allowed to. In a recent production, great angular girders were suspended above the audience so that they could feel something of the menace pressing in on Willy Loman, and as you read the play you must be constantly reminding yourself of the *kind of experience of the setting* that emerges in performance. The world of the play, aspects of its social order and of the protagonist's predicament are often conveyed through the physical details within a framework of theatrical conventions. As you look back through the entire play, note *how* the playwright uses the stage and what sort of demands he makes on his performers in general terms.

(c) *Plot, action and activity*. The link between everyday reality and the way that it is represented on stage in a play is, as we have seen, a rather tenuous one. Sometimes what we see and hear on stage appears to resemble reality so closely that we fail to notice the difference, whereas in other plays the playwright apparently distorts the image to draw attention to a particular point he wishes to make.

Telling a story in the theatre, which is what all plays actually do, is very different from telling it in a novel or narrative poem. The playwright selects events to be shown in a given time and may decide that these events are causally linked or simply acquire significance by being seen in sequence. The action of a play may encompass many years or may occupy precisely the same time as the duration of the play, but, whatever decision the playwright makes concerning time, he must also select the moments in the lives of the characters when the action begins and ends and show us these moments.

Death of a Salesman begins with Willy's arrival home. It is not the only time he has arrived home like this, and yet, in another sense, there has never been a moment like this. *The Caretaker* begins with Mick sitting on the bed looking at a bucket suspended from the ceiling. Very cleverly, Pinter thwarts our expectations by having Mick exit before he has spoken and before we can discover anything about him. Neither playwright has made an arbitrary decision about the starting moment and there is no reason at all why a play should not begin a few seconds before someone gets up and leaves the room. When we study a play, however, we need to examine the impact of the moment when 'the curtain rises'.

Once the action has begun, the plot unfolds. Quite possibly the juxtaposition of events, the coincidences, the carefully contrived suspense and climaxes combine to create a highly improbable story. But this rarely strikes us in performance; it is more likely to have already struck you in reading. The greatest single problem in reading a play however, is to envisage the action; for example, it is easy to forget the existence of a character if he or she remains silent for a long time. Think of the silent figure of Davies watching and listening to Aston's tremendous speech about his illness. In a performance characters are moving all the time, or if they remain still their very stillness makes a visual statement. Linda's mending of the lining of Willy Loman's jacket or Aston's fiddling with the plug on a toaster are not extraneous details: they arise from the very essence of the story and you must recognise them as something to be investigated as part of a critical response. At a later stage in this book there will be specific suggestions for acquiring a deeper understanding of the movement of a scene, but when you have completed a preliminary reading you ought to be able to identify what the characters are *doing* and *how* the playwright tells the story. Does he, for example, use 'flashback' techniques, as in *Death of a Salesman*, or a simple stage blackout to show a considerable passage of time as in *The Caretaker*?

6   Draw your initial analysis together

You have now read the entire play enough times to satisfy yourself that you could answer questions in a way that shows you have thought about the play under a number of broad headings and can imagine it being performed in the theatre. I hope you now appreciate the important differences between the experiences of reading and theatre-going and will be able to draw upon this understanding for a much closer look at the text. Before you go on to that, it is a good idea to stand back from the play you are studying and to try and draw your thoughts together by asking some simple questions. Can I now see the play as a piece of action to be performed on the stage? Can I see how it deals with tensions and threats to the idea of social order? Have I started to grasp some of the ways in which it is staged? In other words, just run through the topics your first reading should have covered. Sometimes you might find it helpful to discover if the playwright has said anything about the intended effect of the play on stage, but most playwrights, you will find, insist that the meaning of their plays only emerges in performance. A more detailed study of the text, the blueprint for performance, will help establish that meaning, and it is to this problem of more detailed study that I turn in my next chapter.

3

The scene as a
unit for study

ONCE we have established a number of broad, general features
of a play, we are in a position to make a much more detailed
examination of the text. In order to do this we need to break
down the material into manageable units, and in most cases we
can use the 'scene' as the natural division for this purpose. If
you are accustomed to studying Shakespeare, you will
probably think of a 'scene' as being a section of the plot which
takes place at a particular time and location, so that, when
these change, the 'scene' also changes. However, when you
come to study a modern play it is far more helpful to think of
the 'scene' in the way that dramatists of the Restoration period
did: that is, every time a *new character is introduced* there is also a
new '*scene*'. A 'scene', therefore, as our basic unit, is a particular
encounter between a set of characters or even an encounter
between a single character and the audience.

Most modern plays are not printed in acts and scenes. They
are either divided into acts with very obvious divisions into
scenes that are not labelled as such, or they are printed in
scenes without any suggestion of acts. Both Miller's *Death of a
Salesman* and Pinter's *The Caretaker*, for example, are divided
into acts without numbered scenes, whereas the plays of Brecht
are invariably a series of scenes. Act I of *Death of a Salesman* itself
falls naturally into some fifteen scenes and it's a good idea to
begin your detailed study of a text by identifying these small
units. This will provide you with manageable chunks of the text
to look at help to focus your analysis.

As we have seen, there is a substantial difference between
the form in which Shakespeare's plays have come down to us
and the appearance of a modern play. A first glance at the
opening pages of *The Caretaker* or *Death of a Salesman* or *Look*

Back in Anger shows them to be dense with comprehensive descriptions of the stage setting and instructions to the performers. Indeed, the detail with which a modern playwright notates his intentions can make the reading of the text a very slow process. If you come to modern drama from having worked on Shakespeare, with his minimal stage directions and no additional indications of how lines are to be spoken except punctuation, you might be tempted to ignore the stage directions. It is, however, vital that you do read these, otherwise you will fail to grasp much of the particular force of the play you are studying. If you are unsure why this should be so, I suggest you quickly reread the introductory chapter to this book where I have explained the particular characteristics of a modern play and why so much more attention is now paid to such features as setting and the movement of characters.

To illustrate these characteristics and their implications for close study I am going to take the first two pages from a famous play which dates from 1879, the early part of the 'modern' period when theatre technology had reached a high level of sophistication and when the forces operating in middle-class society were very like those of today: Ibsen's **A Doll's House**.* The play concerns the apparently happy marriage between the attractive Nora and her husband Torvald, who has recently been promoted to a good position in a bank. Torvald is infatuated with Nora and treats her like a beautiful doll whilst maintaining a strict moral tone in his household. Unbeknown to him, Nora has borrowed money and forged Torvald's signature in order to pay for a holiday which he needed when he was seriously ill. Nora has secretly earned money to repay this debt to a money-lender, Krogstad, who begins to blackmail Nora into pressing her husband to join him in a post in the bank. Torvald's reaction to the discovery of Nora's intrigue reveals attitudes which Nora can no longer tolerate, particularly since she has now experienced a sense of independence by earning money. The marriage disintegrates.

A first reading of the play might lead you to spot that the play is concerned with a tension between freedom and restraint. There is a sense that family life is ordered by artificial

* The translation quoted below is by Michael Meyer, as printed in Ibsen, *Plays: Two* (Methuen, 1980). The quotations are from pp. 23–5.

and narrow codes. The object of your then looking in far greater detail at a particular scene is to fill out your impression and to see how Ibsen brings the play to life. A good scene to start with is the first. We are told in the list of characters that Torvald Helmer is a lawyer and that Nora is his wife; the action takes place in the Helmers' apartment. We then have the following detailed description of the setting:

> *A comfortably and tastefully, but not expensively furnished room. Backstage right a door leads to the hall; backstage left, another door to* HELMER's *study. Between these two doors stands a piano. In the middle of the left-hand wall is a door, with a window downstage of it. Near the window, a round table with armchairs and a small sofa. In the right-hand wall, slightly upstage, is a door; downstage of this, against the same wall, a stove lined with porcelain tiles, with a couple of armchairs and a rocking-chair in front of it. Between the stove and the side door is a small table. Engravings on the wall. A what-not with china and other bric-à-brac; a small bookcase with leather-bound books. A carpet on the floor; a fire in the stove. A winter day.*

Three features should strike you. First, what this room tells you about the Helmers. Ibsen is quite specific that the room is comfortably but *not* expensively furnished; clearly the Helmers enjoy a very adequate standard of living but they are not affluent. The playwright also indicates that they are people of some sensitivity by the *taste* with which the room is furnished, and we further learn that music and books play a part in their lives through the presence of the piano and leather-bound volumes. In real life we may make rapid judgements about people's social class, attitudes and tastes simply from the appearance of their homes, and in *A Doll's House* we can form a provisional opinion of Mr and Mrs Helmer before we meet either of them.

Secondly, however, you should have struck by the clear attention to the detail of this environment. Were you to be responsible for a production of the play, you can imagine the trouble you would need to go to in order to comply with all these instructions: a round table, porcelain tiles, china on the what-not, a *real* fire in the stove and so on. Every one of these details makes a visual statement and a contribution to the action and is, therefore, as important as the dialogue. The playwright has taken great care to place his characters in a particular environment with which they can interact.

Thirdly, you will notice the reminders of the fact that the

play is to take place on a stage in a theatre. The doors, windows and furniture are positioned to be seen from an auditorium and their precise locations are defined as upstage (i.e. towards the *back* of the stage), downstage (towards the *front*) or stage right (i.e. to the right of an actor when he is *facing* the audience) and stage left. Additionally, the need for a fire in the stove and the description of the time as '*A winter day*' will remind you that such effects must be achieved through the skilled use of stage lighting – a device that was not available to such writers as Shakespeare.

If you are able to make these simple deductions from a paragraph of stage directions you are well on your way to reconstructing the performance imaginatively in your mind and refining your understanding of what I have termed the 'world of the play'. After the opening paragraph of stage setting a second, shorter paragraph initiates the physical action of *A Doll's House* and gives detailed instructions to the actors and actresses:

> *A bell rings in the hall outside. After a moment we hear the front door being opened.* NORA *enters the room, humming contentedly to herself. She is wearing outdoor clothes and carrying a lot of parcels, which she puts down on the table right. She leaves the door to the hall open; through it, we can see a* PORTER *carrying a Christmas tree and a basket. He gives these to the* MAID, *who has opened the door for them.*

The sound of the doorbell and of the door being opened is a necessary reminder of the life outside the room on stage. Many modern plays have their action confined to a single room and their subject matter is, in one sense, domestic, but how the events in that room relate to the outside is of considerable importance too. At this stage, of course, we might not remember that *A Doll's House*, which *begins* with the opening of the door and Nora's cheerful entrance, *ends* with her fateful final exit and the slamming of the door. However, this point illustrates the way in which stage directions are an integral part of the fabric and structure of the play.

First appearances of characters are especially important and you should pay particular attention to these moments. Shaw – another influential modern dramatist – usually gives an extended word portrait of each of the principal characters as they make their first appearances, and, although Ibsen, Miller, Pinter or Osborne do not go to quite these lengths, they do provide substantial material on which the actor or actress can base his or her performance. Details of dress are, like decor, an extension of the personality, and Ibsen very quickly establishes the *mood* of the opening with his instructions for Nora. Compare this with, for example, Miller's instructions for the first entrance of Willy Loman or with Pinter's opening stage directions in *The Caretaker* and notice again how a combination of factors create both an overall atmosphere and a strong initial impression of the protagonists.

A general feeling of optimism and light-heartedness pervades the opening moments of *A Doll's House* and Ibsen quickly explains one of the reasons – the approach of Christmas. With her first words, Nora reinforces a sense of suppressed excitement and this flows over into her generosity to the Porter, to whom she gives two and a half times as much as he had asked for. The tiny incident of the tipping of the Porter very quickly acquires significance in the rest of the play as Nora's handling of money becomes a serious issue: again, you might not notice this sort of detail immediately, but do remind yourself that even apparently trivial incidents do have importance and significance in the play.

Ibsen follows the first snippet of dialogue with a further series of instructions for the actress playing Nora:

> NORA *closes the door. She continues to laugh happily to herself as she removes her coat, etc. She takes from her pocket a bag containing macaroons and eats a couple. Then she tiptoes across and listens at her husband's door.*

The optimistic, carefree mood continues; there is something almost childlike in Nora's behaviour. As she 'tiptoes' across to the door, we, the audience, are not to know that it is her husband's study she is approaching, but the moment we hear Helmer's voice we form a judgement of the kind of relationship that exists between them. Like Nora's conduct, it all seems on the level of a game (although, if you know Osborne's *Look Back in Anger*, you may feel uneasy with people who call each other skylarks, squirrels or bears!); in one sense it comes as no surprise when Nora hastily hides the macaroons like a naughty child and there are clear indications of the kind of performance Nora must give us if she is likened to a 'skylark' by Torvald. As many of my students do, you may react with some revulsion to

Torvald's attitude to his wife in the following extract, which forms part of the first 'scene'. I might add here that I divided up Act I of *A Doll's House* into smaller scenes and still found these too long to handle easily, so what I've done is to select a section of the first scene for close analysis. And that is the way to do it: divide the play into scenes, choose a scene for analysis, then, if necessary, take an extract from a scene for closer discussion. The first scene is always a good example to use, just because you will find it crowded with helpful stage directions and pointers about the characters. Looking at the first scene will normally provide you with a solid sense of the play which you can then build on by looking at other scenes.

NORA. Hide that Christmas tree away, Helen. The children mustn't see it before I've decorated it this evening. [*To the* PORTER, *taking out her purse*] How much – ?

PORTER. A shilling.

NORA. Here's half a crown. No, keep it.

The PORTER *touches his cap and goes.* NORA *closes the door. She continues to laugh happily to herself as she removes her coat, etc. She takes from her pocket a bag containing macaroons and eats a couple. Then she tiptoes across and listens at her husband's door.*

NORA. Yes, he's here. [*Starts humming again as she goes over to the table, right.*]

HELMER [*from his room*]. Is that my skylark humming out there?

NORA [*opening some of the parcels*]. It is!

HELMER. Is that my squirrel rustling?

NORA. Yes!

HELMER. When did my squirrel come home?

NORA. Just now. [*Pops the bag of macaroons in her pocket and wipes her mouth.*] Come out here, Torvald, and see what I've bought.

HELMER. You mustn't disturb me!

Short pause; then he opens the door and looks in, his pen in his hand.

HELMER. Bought, did you say? All that? Has my little squander-bird been overspending again?

NORA. Oh, Torvald, surely we can let ourselves go a little this year! It's the first Christmas we don't have to scrape.

HELMER. Well, you know, we can't afford to be extravagant.

NORA. Oh yes, Torvald, we can be a little extravagant now. Can't we? Just a tiny bit? You've got a big salary now, and you're going to make lots and lots of money.

HELMER. Next year, yes. But my new salary doesn't start till April.

NORA. Pooh; we can borrow till then.

HELMER. Nora! [*Goes over to her and takes her playfully by the ear.*] What a little spendthrift you are! Suppose I were to borrow fifty pounds today, and you spent it all over Christmas, and then on New Year's Eve a tile fell off a roof on to my head –

NORA [*puts her hand over his mouth*]. Oh, Torvald! Don't say such dreadful things!

HELMER. Yes, but suppose something like that did happen? What then?

NORA. If anything as frightful as that happened, it wouldn't make much difference whether I was in debt or not.

HELMER. But what about the people I'd borrowed from?

NORA. Them? Who cares about them? They're strangers.

HELMER. Oh, Nora, Nora, how like a woman! No, but seriously, Nora, you know how I feel about this. No debts! Never borrow! A home that is founded on debts and borrowing can never be a place of freedom and beauty. We two have stuck it out bravely up to now; and we shall continue to do so for the few weeks that remain.

NORA. [*goes over towards the stove*]. Very well, Torvald. As you say.

So far we've looked at the setting of *A Doll's House*, at the instructions Ibsen gives his actors and actresses at the start of the play, and at the appearance of Nora and the opening mood. Now we can look at how Ibsen shows Nora and Helmer together. Helmer's first appearance is a carefully prepared entrance. Notice how precisely Ibsen envisages it in performance: the first rather 'blanket' remark from inside the door, showing that, at best, he's only been half listening; the pause and *then* the entrance as he realises what Nora has just said. The first impression we have of Torvald is that he is at work; he comes out with his pen in his hand, he is obviously some kind of professional man who works at home, and, although the rest of his family (did you notice how economically Ibsen tells us there are children?) may be relaxing, *he* is working. The husband and wife roles seem pretty clearly defined: loving, solid, rather sombre husband; attractive, fluttering, rather irresponsible wife. It may be possible to speak Torvald's lines tongue-in-cheek, but they do have a serious edge to them. He is clearly concerned that there must not be extravagance and, after all, the audience has been shown clearly in the details of the setting that the Helmers are not wealthy and they have seen examples of Nora's ways with money that Torvald has not seen.

Soon, however, the context of Nora's behaviour is established. Ibsen feeds a vital piece of information into what could become a simple clash of the personalities. This is a very sensitive domestic situation which is familiar in middle-class society: the husband has got promotion. In anticipation of the larger salary Nora feels able to relax what has obviously been a tight budget. It is invariably at such times as Christmas that the need to economise and 'scrape' hits especially hard, so it is inevitable that Nora, who probably bore the brunt of such economisings at Christmas, should feel as she does. Torvald appears to take a joyless but possibly more realistic view, and we can see in the divergence of their views a source of tension between the characters and a hint of their respective predicaments.

We should remember that at the time this play was written the attitude to borrowing money was more guarded than in our credit-card age, although the pressures that such borrowing bring are probably no less acute now. Nora's suggestion 'we can borrow till then' certainly has something of the 'live now, pay later' mentality that suggests a desire to break out of a restraint that has become tedious. Helmer, given the precise instruction to take her by the ear as an authoritarian schoolmaster might, obviously feels that Nora is too reckless and too unwilling to look to the future. His comment 'how like a woman' would be regarded by most people today as totally unacceptable and, indeed, *A Doll's House* is regarded as an important contribution to the cause of women's rights in the nineteenth century; but notice how Ibsen uses this moment to establish the social order which Nora already appears to threaten. Man is the provider, the planner for the future; there must be no debts; the home is the foundation of society, a place of beauty and freedom.

This unit of the scene concludes with an important stage direction which changes the whole mood. There is resignation in what Nora says, but you should ask yourself 'why does she move over to the stove?' The best way to discover is to try acting out this short scene yourself and you will soon discover why you feel you must move away from Torvald at this point: there will be detailed suggestions for this type of discovery through activity in Chapter 6. Nora's *motivation* for this activity is her unease and, possibly, her irritation. Something about Torvald's attitude and what he has said clearly upsets her. The actress playing Nora in a full-scale production will know the entire play and will have discovered significant facts about Nora's past which actually contribute to her reaction at this point. Your answer to the question 'Why does Nora move to the stove?' would also be different if you knew the whole play, which is why I have suggested that you should have got to know the play in general terms *before* you attempt such detailed study. However, in some examination situations you may be required to comment in some detail on an extract from a play you have not read. In that case you are like a member of the audience who sees Nora move and must decide at that moment why she does. That move introduces an unexpected element of tension into the scene; it not only changes the joyous mood of the opening, but also suggests that Nora could quickly tire of her game of skylarks, although, at this point, she seems to also be making a gesture of submission to her authoritarian husband.

You may by now be feeling overwhelmed by what I am expecting you to dig out from a short extract; and you may feel somewhat confused that we have so far made little mention of the actual language of the play. Do be reassured that any literate person can make the kind of deductions I have made here, provided that he or she thinks of the play in question as a totality, as something seen and acted and not just as dialogue. It *does* get much easier with experience and there *does* come a point when you need to focus specifically on the language. Before you reach that stage, however, there are some important matters concerning a short unit or scene on which you should reflect.

The extract which I have looked at is about the right length for you to consider initially. If you look at all the physical actions in the scene, such as the moment when Nora puts the macaroons in her pocket, the moment when Torvald takes her playfully by the ear or when Nora moves over to the stove, you will notice that these are all key moments which mark a significant if small change of mood or reveal some fact or attitude. Spotting these key moments will soon come quite easily to you and will help you to determine the pattern of a scene such as this. Looking back over it now you can detect a definite shape in its construction. Put simply, the tension gradually rises from a totally relaxed to a somewhat edgy mood. You should now be able to identify the stages by which it rises – these are key moments when the pace of the scene slackens and quickens. The playwright gives us pauses, longer and shorter patches of dialogue and some music (Nora's humming), all of which create a particular mood and impression. We are also given a great deal of information.

Coming at the opening of the play, this is part of the *exposition* in which the playwright lays out the situation from which we may expect a major complication to arise. It is quiet remarkable just how much we do know after this couple of pages – you should feel that you have a very clear idea of what is going on here. Ibsen, and many of the modern playwrights who followed him, took great care with this aspect of their work and the result is that we are given an insight into character.

To reinforce and extend what we have considered so far, I would suggest that you take the initial unit of **Death of a Salesman** as a further working example, looking in turn at the setting and instructions for the actors and characters. As you may remember, *Death of a Salesman* is about a travelling salesman, Willy Loman, who is exhausted by the demands of his job and bitterly disappointed in his two sons, Happy and Biff, who have both failed to live up to the American Dream of success. The play opens with Willy's homecoming after a particularly frustrating day and his wife, Linda, is already in bed. The first unit ends with Willy's first exit from the bedroom. Miller was a great admirer of Ibsen; he even made a special adaptation of one of Ibsen's plays, *An Enemy of the People*, so we may expect to find influences of Ibsen's techniques here. The detail and scope of the first stage directions are reminiscent of *A Doll's House*: Miller takes great care to establish a particular mood and gives precise instructions as to how the stage space is to be transformed to convey a large quantity of information and to create an environment for the action. Prior to Willy's entrance, which takes us very quickly into the world of the play and makes us keenly aware of his predicament, Miller employs music to make another kind of impression on the audience. Once you have studied all the details of the setting and the characters in the way I have outlined for the Ibsen extract, you should think carefully about the flute and its significance.

Your study of this extract will follow a number of more general readings of the play and so you may recall that this is not the only use of music. At other points Miller has specified '*A single trumpet note*', '*raw, sensuous music*', '*idyllic music*', '*a single cello string*', using music with the same type of awareness as a film-producer. Each of these instructions rewards your attention, but the flute is a recurring motif. Notice when it dies away and returns in the first scene and how it is used throughout the play; it reasserts its music in the final moments of the play as if the idea which it represents is as important at the end as at the opening. Obviously, there is a link with the fact that Willy's father was a maker of flutes: it is as if the melody of the flutes of the past has woven a web round Willy's mind so that he cannot escape. You will notice how it is at the frightening moment in the first scene when Willy realises he is still living in the past that the *'flute is heard distantly'*.

The music is one of a number of *images* which the playwright introduces to give greater significance to the action. At one level *Death of a Salesman* appears to be a naturalistic play with a degree of pictorial realism about the stage setting and credible behaviour by believable characters, but at another level what we see and hear constitute powerful images that make more complex statements. Instead, that is, of presenting us just with a 'slice of life' on stage, Miller uses the play's music-imagery to express Willy's feeling of being caught up in intangible, haunting events that cannot be explained. It is precisely because we come to modern plays with an expectation that they will be like 'slices of life' that anything which works against this is so disturbing.

In this 'exposition' part of the play we usually expect to learn a good deal about the characters. Notice particularly how these details are established; what the playwright tells us directly in stage directions; what he tells us indirectly by the way they move, talk and react; what one character says about another – there are excellent examples of all three modes in this scene. Try to ascertain the motives for the characters' actions as indicated in stage directions; why, for example does Willy start to put on his jacket but Linda take it from him?

We have seen both in this scene and in the extract from *A Doll's House* how important a moment a character's entrance is, but you should give equal attention to *exits*. The first scene of Act I of *Death of a Salesman* concludes with Willy's leaving the bedroom. One of his reasons for doing so is that he is going to get himself something to eat. Earlier in the scene there has been some talk of a cheese sandwich and Linda has tried to bring Willy's mind back to the subject whenever his distress has seemed to be dominating his attitude. By the time Willy does leave the room, his exhaustion and Linda's reaction to it appear to have complex causes and elements of self-deception, so that we are left wondering if Willy perhaps leaves the room because he cannot continue the conversation. His final words, 'Close your eyes, I'll be right up', indicate concern for Linda but also a wish that she shouldn't try to intrude too deeply into his world. Conversely, Linda's 'Be careful on the stairs, dear! The cheese is on the middle shelf' is an apparently matter-of-fact utterance which shows equal concern but, perhaps, an unwillingness to confront the real issues. Significantly, Linda does *not* close her eyes or go to sleep but leaves the bedroom.

In rehearsal a director would probably work for some while to achieve the most effective and powerful exit from the actor playing Willy. This is something that you can explore in practical terms too, but if this is not possible you must attempt to visualise Willy's movements for clues to his state of mind. You ought also at this stage to be able to summarise what the audience has learned about Willy during this first scene: it is a significant amount.

Both *A Doll's House* and *Death of a Salesman* lend themselves fairly easily to the sort of rational analysis I have suggested before. Analysing a scene in a play, however, is not always as easy as this, although exactly the same moves will help you. In Pinter's *The Caretaker*, for example, you might find that after your first reading of the play you know no more than that it is a play about a tramp, Davies, who is brought home by one brother, Aston, but forced to leave by another, Mick. If you remind yourself of the way all plays tend to deal with a broad tension betweeen the idea of social order and the reality of life's disorder, you might start to make some further sense of the action. But your grasp of the play is only really going to grow firm if you look at the text, if you do tackle a scene, or at least a section of a scene. That is what I am going to do now and I'm going to take the opening of **A Taste of Honey** (1958) written by Shelagh Delaney when she was a seventeen-year-old schoolgirl. As with the opening of Ibsen's play, I shall look at *setting, instructions,* and *characters* to see what emerges.

A Taste of Honey is about a seventeen-year-old girl, Jo, who lives with her mother, Helen, in a dreary flat in Manchester. Helen, described as a '*semi-whore*', has had several affairs and leaves Jo to live with her latest boyfriend. In her absence, Jo becomes pregnant by a young sailor and then develops a friendship with a gentle, homosexual boy, Geof. Helen returns after the failure of her recent relationship and the play ends with mother and daughter bickering on equal terms. Much of the interest of the play lies in the tension between Jo and her mother and in her relationship with Geof. Here are the opening moments of the play:

> *The stage represents a comfortless flat in Manchester and the street outside. Jazz music. Enter* HELEN, *a semi-whore, and her daughter,* JO. *They are loaded with baggage.*
>
> HELEN. Well! This is the place.
> JO. And I don't like it.
> HELEN. When I find somewhere for us to live I have to consider something far more important than your feelings . . . the rent. It's all I can afford.
> JO. You can afford something better than this old ruin.
> HELEN. When you start earning you can start moaning.
> JO. Can't be soon enough for me. I'm cold and my shoes let water . . . what a place . . . and we're supposed to be living off her immoral earnings.
> HELEN. I'm careful. Anyway, what's wrong with this place? Everything in it's falling apart, it's true, and we've no heating – but there's a lovely view of the gasworks, we share a bathroom with the community and this wallpaper's contemporary. What more do you want? Anyway it'll do for us. Pass me a glass, Jo.
> JO. Where are they?
> HELEN. I don't know.
> JO. You packed 'em. She'd lose her head if it was loose.
> HELEN. Here they are. I put 'em in my bag for safety. Pass me that bottle – it's in the carrier.
> JO. Why should I run round after you? [*Takes whisky bottle from bag.*]
> HELEN. Children owe their parents these little attentions.
> JO. I don't owe you a thing.
> HELEN. Except respect, and I don't seem to get any of that.
> JO. Drink, drink, drink, that's all you're fit for. You make me sick.
> HELEN. Others may pray for their daily bread, I pray for . . .
> JO. Is that the bedroom?
> HELEN. It is. Your health, Jo.
> JO. We're sharing a bed again, I see.
> HELEN. Of course, you know I can't bear to be parted from you.
> JO. What I wouldn't give for a room of my own! God! It's freezing! Isn't there any sort of fire anywhere, Helen?
> HELEN. Yes, there's a gas-propelled thing somewhere.
> JO. Where?
> HELEN. Where? What were you given eyes for? Do you want me to carry you about? Don't stand there shivering; have some of this if you're so cold.
> JO. You know I don't like it.
> HELEN. Have you tried it?

JO. No.

HELEN. Then get it down you! [*She wanders around the room searching for fire.*] 'Where!' she says. She can never see anything till she falls over it. Now, where's it got to? I know I saw it here somewhere . . . one of those shilling in the slot affairs; the landlady pointed it out to me as part of the furniture and fittings. I don't know. Oh! It'll turn up. What's up with you now?

JO. I don't like the smell of it.

HELEN. You don't smell it, you drink it! It consoles you.

JO. What do you need consoling about?

HELEN. Life! Come on, give it to me if you've done with it. I'll soon put it in a safe place. [*Drinks.*]

JO. You're knocking it back worse than ever.

HELEN. Oh! Well, it's one way of passing time while I'm waiting for something to turn up. And it usually does if I drink hard enough. Oh my God! I've caught a shocking cold from somebody. Have you got a clean hanky, Jo? Mine's wringing wet with dabbing at my nose all day.

JO. Have this, it's nearly clean. Isn't that light awful? I do hate to see an unshaded electric light bulb dangling from the ceiling like that.

HELEN. Well, don't look at it then.

JO. Can I have that chair, Helen? I'll put my scarf round it.

[JO *takes chair from* HELEN, *stands on it and wraps her scarf round light bulb – burning herself in the process.*]

(Methuen, 1959, pp. 7–9)

The setting demands a multi-focus design in which the interior of the flat and the street outside are both visible. From the first few speeches onwards the stage directions' description of the flat as '*comfortless*' is reinforced. Jo calls it a 'ruin', Helen says 'Everything in it's falling apart'; we learn that there is inadequate heating and that there is an unshaded light-bulb and a view of the gasworks. Other details of comparative squalor emerge. Jo and Helen must share a bed and share a bathroom with other tenants; the cold permeates the action, as Jo shivers and Helen makes a vain attempt to search for a gas fire.

In this opening extract, then, there is a strong emphasis on the discomfort of the environment which Jo and Helen have just entered. We learn that this is rented accommodation and that Helen has made the arrangements. Whereas she remains somewhat unaffected by the place, the effect on Jo, who longs for a room of her own, is utterly depressing. We can tell from Jo's reaction to having to share her mother's room and bed that she has been frequently shifted from one unpleasant piece of temporary accommodation to another.

The instructions to the two actresses performing the scene are of two kinds: specific stage directions and indications for activities in the text itself. The scene begins with the two characters entering, loaded with baggage and the subsequent action revolves around the feeling of the strangeness of the new home and the fact that neither knows where anything is, either in the flat or in the baggage. Jo stands around shivering in her wet shoes and is ordered about by Helen, who is desparate for a drink. All of Jo's activities are a reaction to her situation; she is unwilling to do anything and stands sniffing a glass of whisky thrust into her hand by Helen, unable to drink it. Her only positive movement is her attempt to mask the glare of the unshaded light-bulb by wrapping her scarf round it. This totally impracticable solution simply results in her burning herself. Whereas Jo remains largely static in the scene, grudgingly taking orders from her mother and doing everything possible to demonstrate her discomfort, Helen is mainly concerned to find her whisky bottle and the glasses. She wanders around the room, drinks a great deal, tries to force Jo to drink and then snatches the glass from her in annoyance, sniffs, gets a clean handkerchief from Jo and generally disregards the setting in favour of responding to her own immediate needs.

The activities of the two characters bring out various forms of tension. There is the tension between mother and daughter and the tension between each character and the environment. When Helen and Jo first enter, the audience does not know that they are mother and daughter, although their age difference should suggest this; however, their precise relationship is quickly confirmed in Helen's comment, 'Children owe their parents these little attentions'. Nevertheless, from the start, the tensions between them is apparent. Helen has provided the home, she is the one who is earning and Jo is deemed to have no right to complain while she is not earning. The nature of Helen's earnings further heightens the potential for tension between the two. Mother and daughter argue, insult each other and spar around with their relationship. One moment Helen is Jo's mother, seeking respect, the next moment Jo simply calls her Helen. They both have a sense of irony, but Jo has the more waspish tongue, watching her mother drink herself into degradation.

This opening extract shows the threat of disorder in a situation where the idea of social order can be detected. There is, obviously, affection between mother and daughter. Given the obvious absence of a father, Helen has provided a home and has to work to do so. But the actuality is that Jo is denied the sort of home and privacy that a seventeen-year-old might reasonably hope for. The nature of her mother's lifestyle, the environment and the needs of adolescence have left her without physical or emotional support and she is clearly vulnerable. The relationship between mother and daughter seems too equal for comfort and traditional roles are upset. Whereas a daughter might wish to move gradually towards independence against a background of love and support, here she is both forced and anxious to achieve it.

One further detail of the scene to be considered is the use of jazz music as an introduction. The music sets the scene in the period of the 1950s, a time when jazz clubs and 'pop' music were establishing themselves as a central feature of teenage culture in Britain. The use of jazz here is doubly significant: it suggests something about Helen and Jo's lifestyle; and it acts as a symbol of an increasingly independent younger generation. In the original production, characters danced on and off the stage in later scenes, giving the play a strange dreamlike, escapist quality at odds with its harsh realities.

You might like to look back now at the comments I made on the setting, instructions to performers and the characters of *A Doll's House* to make an interesting comparison. Notice the relative comfort of Ibsen's middle-class environment as opposed to the bleakness of Shelagh Delaney's Manchester flat; look at the ideals of secure family life as hinted at by both dramatists and the instructions for the performers as the playwrights introduce their characters and their environments to the audience.

One further feature of a scene should concern you at this stage. We have seen how the dramatist makes use of the stage *space*, changing its appearance with scenery and lighting and determining the characters' entrances and exits; but there is also the question of *time*. In the theatre time can be manipulated: an act which in reality lasts forty minutes may embrace the events of several hours; for example, in the first act of *The Caretaker* a simple blackout of a few seconds represents the passage of the night. During a short scene darkness may fall or some quite substantial event may be assumed to have taken place offstage. It is important, then, to recognise how time is being used in any scene which you are studying. Some scenes can create the impression of time passing very slowly, while others may be so full of events that time appears to be accelerated. A single scene may contain several devices for the shaping of time, but it is the temporal relationship of one scene to another which determines the structure and style of a play.

In *Death of a Salesman* Arthur Miller uses a 'flashback' technique so that certain scenes take place at a period earlier than the main body of the play. This technique has become familiar through film and television and is not unknown in novels, yet it has a particular power in the theatre. Modern drama has continually explored the idea that characters are a product of their past, and for the audience suddenly to be transported into that past enables them to view subsequent events in an entirely different way. Pinter has recently experimented with this idea in his play *Betrayal*, where each consecutive scene takes place at an earlier time than the scene preceding it – we begin at the end of the story and end with its beginning, so to speak. Willy, in *Death of a Salesman*, is constantly troubled by the past and yet he seems to live in it, so the scenes of the past are almost more 'real' than those of the present.

Notice how each scene you study relates to the next. In a play by Brecht the lapse may be undefined, very large or minimal; in an Ibsen play the action of an entire act is likely to be continuous and the act separated by a clearly defined time lapse. Observe the complete time span of a play and how that relates to the real time which a performance would occupy and the contribution of each scene to the whole. The playwright's intentions will dictate his use of time, so that, for instance, Brecht will present events so that they do not seem causally linked whereas Ibsen shows the present as inextricably bound up with the past. The interest which the audience takes in accounting for characters' behaviour with reference to their past experiences is once again frustrated by such plays as *The Caretaker* or *Waiting for Godot*. In these plays the past seems threatening, painful but often hazy. Memory, which is so vivid in *Death of a Salesman*, becomes unreliable, so that both time past and the future are very uncertain, if not meaningless.

We have looked at the detail contained in a scene without closely considering the nature of the language which the playwright has created for his characters to speak. Obviously our account of a play is not going to stand up unless we do look at its language and focus on its detail. Once you have thought carefully about the action and shape of a scene, then, you should turn your attention to the language; this will constitute a further stage in your study of the play, and also the topic of the next chapter.

4

Looking at the language of plays

PLAYS normally consist of people doing and saying things in a fashion that is carefully contrived by the dramatist. If a play were simply to consist of action with no speech or speech without action, we should find it unsatisfactory, although there are modern plays which explore both these possibilities. Some of Samuel Beckett's plays, for instance, consist of characters who speak but are entirely static, whereas Anthony Shaffer's play *Murderer* begins with half an hour of silent action. Normally, however, we expect the action and the dialogue of a play to be interrelated, one advancing the other. In some older forms of drama both action and language where highly stylised, but the majority of modern plays rely for their effect on a mode of behaving and speaking which the audience immediately recognises as being like that of everyday life. This has particularly been true in the case of theatre language ever since Ibsen abandoned writing plays in verse in favour of what he called the 'very much more difficult art of writing the genuine plain language spoken in real life'.

To suggest that playwrights since Ibsen have attempted merely to imitate everyday speech is an over-simplification, for, clearly, just to use everyday language would be tedious, trivial and lacking in any form of dramatic interest. A playwright is not engaged in pure imitation but rather like a TV comic who impersonates various famous people, he or she takes certain characteristics and uses them in such a way that everyone believes in the likeness. In your study of a play you will need to be aware of some of the qualities of language upon which the dramatist has based the dialogue. In order to get to grips with this question of the language of the play, I would suggest that you start by taking a shorter extract as a sample and consider the following four points. It is helpful to keep a checklist of what you discover as you progress.

Language and themes

There are always several reasons why we have to look closely at the language of a play. The dramatist's language serves to bring the play's action to life just as it also serves to bring the characters to life and to create a sense of the world they inhabit. I shall expand on all of these areas later, but the point I want to stress here is, in a way, much more obvious. What students sometimes fail to grasp is that the language of a play also serves to bring the play's themes to life. When you look at a scene or an extract from a play, you should be able to make a connection between the words spoken and the themes or issues your initial analysis and reading of the play have established as important. For example, in Chapter 2 I suggested how an initial reading of Miller's *Death of a Salesman* might lead us towards seeing how the play is concerned with the gap between social harmony and the painful reality of life where men such as Willy Loman battle with failure. If you were studying Miller's play you would, by this stage of your analysis, have looked at a number of scenes to establish how Miller presents this large theme and creates his powerful, moving drama. But your analysis might remain rather vague unless you had also turned to the play's language to examine how it serves to voice Miller's theme. In the second half of this chapter I shall be discussing a 'key' speech from *Death of a Salesman* to illustrate this point more fully, so perhaps here I can give you an example from a different sort of play.

In Bertolt Brecht's **Mother Courage and her Children** (first seen in Britain in 1955), we see a woman and her children making their way across Europe during war by selling provisions to the fighting armies. Even without any more details than this, you should be able to begin to see how the short extract below (from scene 4) serves to illuminate the play's theme of war. As with all such extracts, the best way to gain an insight into how the language works is to bear in mind the idea of a tension or contrast between an idea of order and the reality of life's disorder, or between an idea of something positive and something negative. This contrast will provide you with a link between the play as a whole and the detail of its language. Here, first is the extract:

> THE CLERK. I know you. You had a paymaster from the Lutherans with you, what was in hiding. I'd not complain if I were you.
> MOTHER COURAGE. But I got a complaint to make. I'm innocent, would look as how I'd a bad conscience if I let this pass. Slashed everything in me cart to pieces with their sabres, they did, then wanted I should pay five taler fine for nowt, I tell you, nowt.
> CLERK. Take my tip, better shut up. We're short of canteens, so we let you go on trading, specially if you got a bad conscience and pay a fine now and then.
> MOTHER COURAGE. I got a complaint.
> CLERK. Have it your own way. Then you must wait till the captain's free.
> (tr. John Willet, Methuen, 1980, p. 43)

Mother Courage is waiting outside the captain's tent to complain about damage to her cart. In that detail alone, in her words about how the soldiers 'Slashed everything in me cart to pieces', we get a sense of the horrifying violence of war and its wanton destructiveness. Clearly this is the negative side of the scene and it's not hard to see how these details help to create a sense of the chaos of war. What, though, can we set against this idea? We should, I've said, be able to spot some sort of tension in the scene. Well, Mother Courage wants justice: she talks about being innocent, about having a 'conscience'. If you think about this, you should be able to see how the scene turns upon the contrast between the idea of the chaos of war and the idea of an ordered society where justice and innocence prevail. In the play itself such a scheme of things is shown to be remote – society is too busy making war and money to bother about justice and innocence – but it is scenes such as this which bring these ideas to life. Of course, the language of any scene operates on several levels at once, so that besides bringing the themes to life it also brings the characters to life, which leads me on to the next point.

Language of character

When we speak of a 'character' in a play we think of them as a living person but, in reality, until an actor begins to work on the play the character is nothing more than a series of speeches and stage directions on the page. What a character says and how he or she says it are major features of bringing a play to life and will determine the way in which a performer conceives the person he or she is portraying. In everyday life we associate people with particular characteristics of speech, such as a tendency to talk a lot or to use certain peculiar phrases. The same applies to plays, and your first task in a study of dialogue is to *try and identify the speech characteristics of each character*. Look at almost any page of John Osborne's *Look Back in Anger* and you will notice that if Jimmy Porter, the central character, is on stage he is doing most of the talking. In the first moment of the play Jimmy complains to his wife, Alison, and their friend Cliff, 'You bet you weren't listening. Old Porter talks, and everyone turns over and goes to sleep'; but as the play progresses we begin to understand why. Jimmy, who is exceedingly articulate and speaks with the fluency of a highly educated person, simply talks too much and talks *at* people rather than *to* them. However, we only begin to understand his character when we appreciate the frustration he feels at not finding an audience who will listen. Harold Pinter's *The Caretaker* is another play in which people do not listen to each other, but here the characters have quite different characteristics. In this play Aston, who has at one time been a patient in a psychiatric hospital, rescues a tramp, Davies, from a brawl and brings him to his home. Davies keeps talking even when he has nothing to say and uses highly repetitive speech patterns, whereas Aston's brother Mick uses smart, slick talk to intimidate Davies. Aston himself, however, uses language in such a measured and tentative way that when he delivers a massive monologue about the mental hospital it comes as a great theatrical shock.

Where characters spend a great deal of time in conversation, as in Tom Stoppard's *Rosencrantz and Guildenstern are Dead* or Beckett's *Waiting for Godot*, it is particularly important, though sometimes difficult, to notice how the characters are differentiated in the dialogue. If you get into the habit of reading the plays aloud you will, however, be able to detect the varying vocabulary, patterns and rhythms that characterise one person rather than another. Watch out for characters who invariably speak in monosyllables or in short, staccato phrases; others may use long, rounded sentences and others will never finish a sentence. This is where similarities to everyday speech are fascinating and crucial, because in spoken language we rarely use the complete sentences we would write. Many aspiring playwrights make this mistake and give their characters the kind of spoken sentences you would find in an essay, and the results seem highly contrived and artificial. That is the difference between a 'speech' which might be written down and delivered on some formal occasion and a 'speech' from a play which represents somebody talking spontaneously.

In everyday situations we usually make judgements on people from the way they speak, and part of the process of studying the language of a play involves us in determining not only what judgements we have formed from a particular character's use of language but also what judgements other characters in the play would have formed. Under this heading, therefore, you will be looking for clues to educational and class background, place of origin, attitudes, level of confidence, self-esteem, skill in communication, ability to calm or persuade other people, and so on. Eventually you will discover that each character has his or her distinctive 'voice' and that much of the important differentation between characters is achieved through language. You should make a note of all these features as they occur to you.

Language, thought and action

When you examine the characters of a play it is useful to think of them as adopting various strategies to achieve certain goals. Insights into the motives of characters are provided by the words they speak. Early in Miller's *Death of a Salesman* Biff, one of Willy the salesman's sons, explains why he has come home. The length of Biff's speeches, the meandering from one thought to another, confirms what his mother Linda says of him: 'I think he's very lost.' Willy, however, uses language to convince himself that what he and Linda really know to be true is not the case. One moment he exclaims, 'Biff is a lazy bum!' but a few seconds later he says, 'There's one thing about Biff, he's not lazy.' Following this extraordinary self-contradiction, Willy, whose life as a salesman has become intolerable, goes on to reminisce, to escape from the present into the past. Characters in plays often use language for the purpose of avoiding reality, whereas at other times they may try to come to terms with a situation by verbalising their deepest thoughts. The next stage, then, in your study of a characters' language is to *identify the purpose for which language is being used*.

In order to do this you need to think about the way in which language is *normally* used. We often use words to express our thoughts, but sometimes to conceal our thoughts. We may speak in an attempt to establish a relationship or hide the fact that we are feeling awkward. We may say precisely the opposite of what we feel in order to achieve our ends. At times we will resort to polite formalities, jargon or jokes, whereas at other times it may be so important to us to say what we are thinking that we have to prepare ourselves, and even then, perhaps, not really say what we wanted to. We may flatter, sulk, talk excessively, lie, behave charmingly or rudely all to achieve our own ends. Plays which deal with the issues of modern life are bound to use some of these characteristics of language.

Because there is the possibility of a discrepancy between a character's stated ideas and his or her true intentions, actors often describe the words of the play as the 'text' and the motives behind the words as the '*sub text*'. You as a student are forced, like an actor, to study the text in order to discover the sub-text. The idea that something is going on all the time beneath the text is particularly helpful, and you should also bear it in mind when considering the silence that a character employs between speeches. When you are reading a play it is all too easy to forget that the characters carry on thinking and reacting when they are not speaking, and indeed, if they do not speak for some time, it is easy to forget their existence altogether! It is part of your imaginative reconstruction of the play in performance to consider how characters are using periods of personal silence.

Pinter's plays are notable for the pauses which occur between speeches. A great deal has been written concerning Pinter's use of silence, and there is no doubt that in the theatre the intermittent silences have a stunning effect. However, the pauses are more than theatrical silence; they are often an indication that, although two or more people are speaking, they are not communicating. Whereas we normally expect a speech to be a response to a preceding speech by someone else, Pinter's characters often appear to talk along a line of thought governed only by themselves, and the pauses are either a non-response to a previous speech or a period of silent thought preceding another statement. Because plays usually consist of constant dialogue, silence can seem ominous and threatening; so, for example, the two tramps who wait at a roadside in Beckett's *Waiting for Godot* appear to use language as a defence against some kind of ultimate silence and simply to pass the time. This contrasts interestingly with Pinter's *The Caretaker*, with which the play has certain similarities in that Aston and Davies begin their pause-punctuated dialogue in the opening scene by groping towards establishing the basis of their relationship. It is as if each character is tentatively sending up balloons and waiting to see if the other will shoot them down.

You ought also to be able to recognise when characters are using language to overwhelm an opponent. Both Jimmy Porter, who taunts and attacks his wife in *Look Back in Anger*, and Mick, who terrifies the old tramp in *The Caretaker*, do this. They both have a far better cultural background and vocabulary than those with whom they share the stage, but they are also more adroit and flexible in their employment of words. They can intimidate their fellow beings and dictate the whole style and pace of an encounter. Even when Jimmy is self-pitying, he still uses his weakness to focus attention on himself, whereas Mick simply confuses Davies, contradicting himself and deliberately introducing concepts he knows to be beyond Davies's experience. Jimmy enjoys the sound of language and cannot resist the ringing phrase even when he is close to desperation.

We know that conversation can be a very enjoyable activity and we often engage in it for its own sake. It is also the most common means by which we seek to establish relationships, impose our will on others and negotiate to achieve our aims. A play which consisted entirely of pleasureable talk would be extremely boring because nothing would happen, but you will certainly find examples of *all* the possible uses of language in modern drama and invariably they will link with the thoughts of the characters and the actions they play. It is often said by critics that the language of a play should 'advance the action', and this is simply another way of saying that the dialogue has a great deal more than face value; it represents, for example, the major evidence for the protagonist's predicament. By the time you have studied several extracts carefully, you will have become used to recognising the purpose for which language is being used. You may, however, need to go back over earlier extracts to make sure that features you have learned to detect as you become familiar with the idea have not passed unnoticed.

Language and reality

Playwrights following Ibsen's example have been particularly interested in showing accurate representations of human behaviour, and this, inevitably, includes human language. More recently dramatists have been concerned to examine the apparent breakdown of language as an effective means of communication in modern life. All of these areas of concern have led dramatists to provide dialogue which the audience recognises as having the qualities of language used by people in the course of their everyday lives, and in studying a play you should ask *what features of real language are highlighted in the play?* As we have already seen, the language of a play is carefully selected and shaped by the playwright, and by selecting certain features of 'real' dialogue he or she creates the illusion of normal conversation. We readily accept, for example, that the characters in *Death of a Salesman* are conversing normally, yet if you examine almost any of Linda's speeches to her sons Happy and Biff in Act I you will find that they come near to poetry with their repeated patterns of consonants and strong rhythm. Miller has achieved the appearance of reality by using familiar vocabularly and sentence structure and by making Linda's speeches arise from and express her feelings in an entirely believable way, yet he highlights the impact of the structure and form of the language.

Playwrights interested in the weaknesses of language as a means of communication tend to select particular idio-syncrasies of speech. In David Campton's play *Out of the Flying Pan* two delegates arrive from opposite sides of the world, one wearing blue, the other red. For the entire play they converse in high-sounding phrases arising from their ideologies, and although they are ostensibly discussing peace they actually never shift their ground because they do not listen to each other. Their substitute for interaction is the language of diplomacy, a cunning verbal device that conceals real motives in a welter of impressive words. Campton seems to have taken almost all the diplomatic phrases that we might hear on the news or read in the newspaper and condensed them into a play that lasts about forty-five minutes. As with the most successful modern plays, the result is shocking because through the dramatists's artifice we are made to see reality with a frightening clarity.

The use of jargon and of language which conceals rather than communicates is highlighted in a play such as Beckett's *Waiting for Godot*. A character called Lucky delivers an extraordinary and prodigious speech which covers several pages of text. Its impact in the theatre is remarkable, because the experience of listening to it so closely resembles listening to the bombast of politicians and academics! When you read the speech in the text it is utter nonesense: repetitious, garbled and boring. It seems almost incredible that anyone could talk for so long about nothing, and yet we have all felt this about real people at some time or other and had the conviction that there is so much empty jargon that the meaning is lost to anyone but the speaker. When a character in a play speaks publicly but fails to communicate at all, he or she becomes isolated. Beckett's and Pinter's plays are frequently peopled with characters who live an increasingly lonely life, holding a dialogue with themselves.

A need to exploit the features and limitations of language has led modern playwrights to experiment boldly with the use of dialogue. The pattern of dialogue interspersed with soliloquy that may be familiar to you from Shakespeare or the equally spread dialogue of Ibsen may be replaced by pages of rapid monosyllables, such as in the plays of Ionesco or Ann Jellicoe, or the sudden and unexpected speech of enormous length, as in Beckett or Pinter. Pinter is particularly adept at picking up the rhythms and patterns of uneducated English conversation, whereas some of Tom Stoppard's characters seem to converse in clichés.

As you assemble a list of the particular features of 'real' language in your particular play, you may notice that in order to simulate real conversation the playwright may rarely write in complete sentences; instead the dialogue may be frequently interrupted by another speaker and may have strong repetitive elements. You should notice how the dramatist ensures that his characters make their points, remembering that, unlike what happens in the silent reading of a novel or poem, the audience cannot ask an actor to stop and repeat something. The need for dramatic dialogue to make an immediate impact accounts for the care with which each word is chosen as a *spoken* entity, so when you come to make critical appraisal of a playwright's work you are evaluating not the writer's prose style or lyric verse but his or her ability to create powerful and convincing oral communication. If you find this difficult to grasp, read the dialogue aloud and, even better, record yourself doing so.

What, however, are we to make of a modern play such as T. S. Eliot's *Murder in the Cathedral*, a play in verse about the murder of a twelfth-century archbishop of Canterbury? Surely nothing could be further from reality than characters conversing in poetry, some of which is so complex that its meaning is obscure at first hearing. You will no doubt have wrestled with the problems of understanding verse dialogue when studying Shakespeare, but at least then you could attribute the difficulties to the fact that Shakespeare was writing in another age. It may seem almost perverse for a modern playwright to use poetry as dialogue, even if the subject matter of the play is historical – after all, following *Murder in the Cathedral* Eliot went on to write several verse plays in which the physical setting was as contemporary as in a play by Ibsen or Osborne.

Eliot, however, argued that there were levels of reality. On one level a play may seem 'real' if the characters resemble everyday people, are placed in everyday settings, and speak everyday language, but for Eliot this was a surface reality dealing with trivialities and passing events which have little to do with eternal, profound realities. In order to cope with the universal and important truths and themes with which drama should deal, the theatre demanded, Eliot felt, the elevated and richly textured language of poetry. If you are studying an Eliot play you will no doubt wish to discuss whether or not the playwright achieved a balance between language and action in his plays. Some critics and performers would maintain that by focusing entirely upon language Eliot neglected other elements of drama, so that his plays are not entirely successful in the theatre.

T. S. Eliot was nevertheless not really so far from Ibsen's great admirer Arthur Miller as it may first seem. It is, in fact, misleading to think that there are two categories of theatre language: everyday prose, and verse. We have already noted that at times the language of a play such as *Death of a Salesman* has poetic features, some of which help to establish the dreamlike quality of the play, but any modern play, with its carefully orchestrated speeches and sound-effects, may seem like a poem in performance, and your study must include careful attention to the total effect of the spoken language. Individually, the characters in many modern plays, such as those by Beckett, Pinter, Ionesco or Campton, are weak and inarticulate, their language revealing the paltriness of their inner lives, but their struggle against forces which they cannot control will often give the play a sense of poetry that inappropriately 'poetic' language would fail to do.

In their attempts to get closer to realism, British playwrights prior to 1969 felt frustrated and inhibited by the censorship laws, so it is worth checking the date of your 'set' play if it is written by a British playwright. The Lord Chamberlain was empowered to order the excision of any language considered indecent or profane before granting a play a licence for public performance. Playwrights argued that this prevented them from reproducing much of the vitality of the speech of large sections of the population about whom they wished to write; it was no longer acceptable to confine the subject of plays merely to the activities of the upper middle classes with their butlers, gardeners and parlour maids. With the abolition of censorship in 1969, many plays were (and continue to be) written with very accurate simulations of types of language which some people would consider obscene and shocking: Willy Russell's play *Stags and Hens*, set in a ladies' and a gents' lavatory, might be a good example. What is really shocking about this play, however, is the sheer emptiness of the lives of the characters, an emptiness which could certainly not be conveyed so powerfully in all its awfulness without the language. If we are jolted into awareness of something to which the dramatist wants to draw our attention, then the language has done its job.

The theatre may, simply through a pattern of language; bring us in touch with whole cultural groups with which we are unfamiliar; Willy Russell evokes working-class Liverpool, Arnold Wesker the life of rural Norfolk, Harold Pinter the East

End, and Arthur Miller both modern and seventeenth-century New England. As you study the play you should be able to *identify the distinctive qualities of regional language* and relate them to the rhythm of life, the underlying outlook of the people and the cultural expectations of the characters. This requires that you develop an ear for language and that you listen with far greater attention than usual to all kinds of people talking. Listen to conversations in shop queues, in stations and other public places; listen to workmen talking and the incessant talk of radio disc jockeys. How are these people using language? Are they simply filling time, joking, grumbling? If modern drama is concerned with modern life, it is concerned with people such as these, and yet would anyone want to buy a theatre ticket simply to listen to such conversations? The distinction between a work of art and reality has always been debated, and you should be able to explore the difference between a play and a random 'slice of life'.

Key speeches

You have only to try writing a play to discover that there is a great deal more to drama than a succession of speeches, however memorable they may be. The fact remains, though, that the gradual unfolding of a play's ideas and action invariably depends on certain key speeches and that for many people the pleasure of theatre going includes remembering lines that linger in the memory long after the performance has ended. The aptness and power of much theatrical language makes it something to be savoured: Jimmy Porter's startling tirade against women in *Look Back in Anger*, Davies' account of his visit to the monastery in *The Caretaker*, and Beatie's final speech in Wesker's *Roots* are still remembered by those who first heard them and they still make an impact. In some respects these examples show that the most effective dramatic language transcends the 'dated' feeling of much modern drama written only a few years ago, but they show how great speeches *embody key concepts and mark an important moment* in the play. As a final suggestion for the study of language in a play I would recommend, therefore, that you *assemble a list of key speeches* and, if appropriate, memorise both the list and the speeches. Incidentally, a 'speech' may be just a few words.

At almost any point in your study a speech may strike you as being particularly important but the full significance of any speech cannot really be appreciated until you have a fair knowledge of the entire play. If you have followed the steps I have suggested in earlier chapters, this should not pose a problem now. In order to identify a key speech, ask yourself if a speech fulfils some or all of the following criteria.

(a) It appears to sum up or deal with some of the central ideas of the play.
(b) It seems to mark a turning-point in the action so that you can trace events back to the moment of that speech.
(c) It provokes particularly strong emotions in other characters and the audience – laughter, pity, surprise.
(d) It reveals important aspects of a character's motives or attitudes.
(e) It identifies the protagonist's predicament.
(f) You tend to remember it without really trying.

You might feel that it is impossible to apply these criteria because it is such a laborious business remembering them all or constantly checking speeches against the list. However, you will find that, once you have grasped what are the basic characteristics of a key speech, you quickly acquire the skill of identifying such speeches and explaining their importance. You will probably already have noticed that some of the criteria I have listed are so similar to each other that they are virtually indistinguishable, and this is because, in essence, whatever its precise nature, a key speech marks a *significant and identifiable step in the play's development*. Experienced actors and directors recognise such speeches almost instinctively, since they affect performance, and you need to imagine the effect that such a speech will have on the other characters and on the audience.

I may have given you the impression that a play is simply a series of key speeches linked by unimportant speeches. This obviously is not the case. Everything both seen and heard in the theatre has significance, though a play in which every word and line had equal weight would not only be completely intolerable but would also rob the play of essential heightening and relaxation of tension. If you carefully consider all the dialogue in a play lasting, say, two and a half hours, you will find that even the most apparently trite remark has a purpose in the total drama and that, compared with two and a half hours of real life, the language of the play achieves considerably more in terms of interest, shaping events and mounting tension.

Identifying a few key speeches for special consideration, however, gives you the opportunity to look again at the general language characteristics of the play, but this time in greater depth. By the conclusion of your work on key speeches you should be in a position to comment in considerable detail on both the play's action and language in a way that will show a substantial advance on the earlier stages of your study.

Analysing key speeches: a step-by-step guide, with examples

The total process now looks like this. Study the play in manageable units, a few pages at a time. Bearing in mind your knowledge of the whole play, select about six key speeches. If possible, choose speeches by more than one character, but also see that you have more than one speech for the central character. Take the chosen speeches of each character in turn and apply all the questions we have considered in this chapter by using the following steps:

1   *Say in greater detail how the speech embodies a key concept or theme or marks an important moment in the play*
2   *Examine the speech characteristics of the character*
3   *Examine the purpose for which the language is used*
4   *Say what features of real language are being highlighted*
5   *Read the speech aloud and say how the dramatist makes it effective*

Obviously what I'm suggesting here is that, after you've selected your key speeches, you go through the same five basic steps with each speech. So far, though, I have not made any concrete suggestions about how to tackle step 5 – that is, what to look for in a speech when judging its effectiveness. This, however, should become clear in the discussion that follows.

I am now going to suppose that you are continuing to study Arthur Miller's **Death of a Salesman** and that you have reached the stage of selecting a number of what you consider to be key speeches. In order to give you practice and confidence in handling this task, we shall work through a sample speech. You will remember that Willy Loman, a travelling salesman, is desperately weary and unhappy in his job, for which he is temperamentally unsuited. One of the major causes of tension in the play is the profound sense of disappointment that Willy feels in his sons Happy and Biff, for whom he had great ambitions. Linda, Willy's wife, reveals to Happy and Biff that their father, after working for his company for thirty years, has been reduced to selling on straight commission, like a beginner, so that money is now very tight. Biff exclaims, 'Those ungrateful bastards', and the speech I have chosen is Linda's reply. It comes about two-thirds of the way through Act I. I have studied the play in small units and this speech occurs in a section of four and a half pages in which Linda is talking to Biff and Happy. I have defined this section as a unit for study because both before and after it Willy is also on stage. The speech I have chosen is printed below. It is, in fact, the longest speech in the unit, but that does not necessarily make it the most important:

LINDA. Are they any worse than his sons? When he brought them business, when he was young, they were glad to see him. But now his old friends, the old buyers that loved him so and always found some order to hand him in a pinch – they're all dead, retired. He used to be able to make six, seven calls a day in Boston. Now he takes the valises out of the car and puts them back and takes them out again and he's exhausted. Instead of walking he talks now. He drives seven hundred miles, and when he gets there no one knows him any more, no one welcomes him. And what goes through a man's mind, driving seven hundred miles home without having earned a cent? Why shouldn't he talk to himself? Why? When he has to go to Charley and borrow fifty dollars a week and pretend to me that it's his pay? How long can that go on? How long? You see what I'm sitting here and waiting for? And you tell me he has no character? The man who never worked a day but for your benefit? When does he get the medal for that? Is this his reward – to turn around at the age of sixty-three and find his sons, who he loved better than his life, one a philandering bum –

(Penguin, 1961, p. 45)

1 *Say in greater detail how the speech embodies a key concept or theme or marks an important moment in the play*

This speech tells us a great deal more about Willy's predicament than either Happy, Biff or the audience have previously understood and it also reveals far more about Linda. It provokes both surprise and pity and 'turns the tables' in such a way as to shock. It identifies the central issue of the play – the ruthlessness of the consumer society and I find it lingers in my mind. For the first time in the play Linda expresses something of the depth and intensity of her affection for her husband and she is now desperately trying to make her sons appreciate the gravity of the situation and the inappropriateness of their attitudes.

What I think is also evident in this speech is the central tension that runs through the play as a whole, the tension between the idea of harmony and the painful realities of modern American life. Look at how few words in this speech suggest attractive, positive things – 'friends', 'loved' – and set these against the images of life as cruel and indifferent, such as the image of Willy taking his cases out of the car and putting them back again 'exhausted', or the image of Willy driving hundreds of miles and 'no one welcomes him'. Again, look at how the speech simply contrasts the past as enjoyable and successful with the hollow present where Willy has to pretend he is still a great salesman. There is, too, something unbearable about the present, as if there is nothing solid or worthwhile left in Willy's life. Your response to this speech may be very different from mine, but I hope you can see how, just by looking at a few details and relating them to the play's theme, my analysis has progressed and really started to investigate Miller's drama.

2 *Examine the speech characteristics of the character*

Linda tends to speak at greater length than the other characters and she is more reasoned and persuasive in her whole approach. She drives home her points by strong, simple vocabulary and compels people to listen to her. She gives the impression of pent-up energy; hers is 'educated', grammatical speech. Here you should think again of the speech and its context and of your experience of reading it aloud (remember you are really thinking about a character speaking). Imagine how the speech is designed to be spoken – perhaps quickly, loudly, in agitation, excitement, or in some other way; then consider what you imagine to be its effect in the theatre. Ask yourself how the speech of this character differs from that of another character.

3   *Examine the purpose for which the language is used*

Basically Linda wants to change her sons' hideous attitudes, to shake them into a recognition of the truth and to make them confront the reality of the situation. She tries to do this by sharp questions and short, piercing statements. You need to read the speech aloud and explain *how* the dramatist makes it effective: features to look for might include various forms of repetition, perhaps of strongly accentuated words, or maybe in the form of alliteration (several words beginning with the same consonant) or assonance (recurring vowel sounds). Repetition usually achieves emphasis, but this may be of various kinds, and serve different purposes: for example, a character may be trying to drive home a point or expressing disbelief. Look also for questions or images which characters use to make their language move vivid. The *tone* of a speech, often determined by the use of irony, sarcasm and humour, gives a clue to its purpose.

4   *Say what features of real language are being highlighted*

Linda's speech has the flow of a person who is angry and anxious to persuade. There are many questions characteristic of somebody trying to make a strong point, yet the language is simple, everyday vocabulary. This is a mother talking to her sons, so there is a sense of a common language between them; it is uncomplicated and domestic and yet it has the power of a public statement. There are no particular regional features except that both her description of her son as 'a philandering bum' and her expression 'in a pinch' are clearly East Coast American.

　　To identify language features look particularly at the sentence *structure* – are there single, detached sentences containing just one or a few words? Or are there long, complex sentences? Or are these used in combination? You might look also for the use of jargon and dialect here.

5   *Read the speech aloud and say how the dramatist makes it effective*

This is a strong speech built on contrasts – it begins with a surprise accusation of the sons and then compares what was once possible with what is now the case. There is a brittle quality in the alliteration of repeated *b* sounds: 'brought', 'business', 'buyers', yet the sense of a more pleasant past is created by repeated 'old' and the long vowels of 'now', 'loved', 'found', 'order', and suddenly ended by 'dead'. Later in the speech Linda pushes home her point with repeated 'why?' The contrast of past and present is achieved through striking acrimony which also creates a sense of false hope: 'he takes his valises out . . . puts them back . . . takes them out . . . Instead of walking he talks now ' – here the hinted rhyme achieves further contrast and emphasis.

The second half of the speech takes the form of a series of questions of ever-increasing urgency. Linda concludes by rounding on the sons, with whom the speech began. As the speech progresses the sentences become shorter, building the tension, but they are all of relatively simple structure. The tone of the speech is almost rhetorical; it has the art of a public, persuasive speech and it becomes increasingly bitter. There are moments of great pathos as Linda builds a picture of Willy's life and then moves onto the attack.

You can see that the logic of step 5 is to bring together again the issues you have explored in steps 2, 3 and 4. By doing this you will avoid ending up with a very bitty analysis. After reading the speech aloud and thinking about its effect, it's often a good idea to re-examine your response and also to think about the speech as spoken, the other characters' reactions and what happens afterwards. Or you might think further about the character's intentions in delivering the speech, or how it compares with the speeches of other characters. The following paragraph gives some of my own further thoughts about Linda's speech.

The speech gradually accelerates in pace and urgency and probably in volume. Linda may be on the point of breaking down as she reaches the end, but she gives the impression of great control to start with. The speech would be spoken in a calculated almost icy way but there is great emotion in it and this should not be far from the surface. It comes as a shock and we can imagine that it would be heard in silence with great attention – Linda's strength as shown in this speech is surprising and compels attention. Only Happy and Biff are addressed and only they (and the audience) hear. The speech is a reply to Biff's comment on the ingratitude of Willy's employers but both Happy and Biff are indicted. Happy has shown a greater readiness to understand Willy's predicament than Biff but they both have no real concept of his suffering. Biff's reaction is aggressive, as if he is both unable and unwilling to accept the implications of what has been said. Happy makes a single exclamation, 'Mom!' (it is he whom Linda has dismissed as 'a philandering bum'), but he can make no further comment; he seems shocked, deep in thought and in a sense admits that there is no answer.

Linda's intention has been to shock her sons into confronting the gravity of Willy's predicament and she is partially successful. She stings them both into some kind of response, but Linda still has to tell her sons more before they finally realise the full truth. Beneath the text is Linda's lonely carrying of a tremendous burden, the fact of living out a lie, and she can no longer bear it. Thus her frustration and anger come to the surface in this speech. Unlike many of Linda's earlier speeches, in which we feel she is concealing her true feelings, on this occasion she says exactly what she means and retains sufficient control over herself to say it completely. Linda's speech is less colloquial than that of any other speaker; she uses language with sympathy and more control than Willy or her sons. Her words appear to be chosen for maximum effect and they have a greater flow than any of the speeches of the other characters.

The speech itself demands action from Happy and Biff, and their subsequent attitudes and behaviour are shaped by it. In the short term Biff rejects the guilt and there is a growing tension of resentment between the two boys. The most immediate result of the speech is that Linda is forced to tell her sons that she has discovered that Willy is contemplating suicide.

I hope this example will show you the level of attention that you can bring to a key speech. My comments are by no means exhaustive and you may feel that I have missed something you would have mentioned. So much the better. You will notice that I have used all the steps I suggested but within each step have allowed myself considerable flexibility; you should feel free to use the steps as guides, not narrow rules. Further exploration of the language of a play can be achieved in a practical workshop situation, as suggested in Chapter 6. It's likely that thinking about the dramatist's words in the way I have outlined is a new experience for you, and inevitably, it will seem very time-consuming at first. Time spent at this stage, though, will equip you to approach your study with much greater confidence in the future and you will find yourself asking many of the questions almost unconsciously before long. Before going on to the next chapter, however, it may be helpful if I provide one further, very brief example. I have chosen a speech from John Osborne's **Look Back in Anger**.

In this play, Jimmy, a young graduate from a working-class background, is married to Alison, who is from an upper-class family. Jimmy harbours anger and resentment towards Alison's family and this explodes into powerful speeches. Jimmy and Alison share a small flat in a Midland's town with the good-natured Cliff. In the speech which follows, Jimmy is telling Cliff about Alison's brother Nigel while Alison stands passively ironing. It will help you if you quickly look back at the section 'Language and character' (p. 44) before reading it and then remind yourself of the six criteria I suggested for selecting 'key speeches': I think you will find that this speech fulfils them all.

JIMMY [*moving in between them*]. Have you ever seen her brother? Brother Nigel? The straight-backed, chinless wonder from Sandhurst? I only met him once myself. He asked me to step outside when I told his mother she was evil minded.

CLIFF. And did you?

JIMMY. Certainly not. He's a big chap. Well, you've never heard so many well-bred commonplaces come from beneath the same bowler hat. The Platitude from Outer Space – that's brother Nigel. He'll end up in the Cabinet one day, make no mistake. But somewhere at the back of that mind is the vague knowledge that he and his pals have been plundering and fooling everybody for generations. [*Going upstage, and turning*.] Now Nigel is just as vague as you can get without being actually invisible.

And invisible politicians aren't much use to anyone – not even to *his* supporters! And nothing is more vague about Nigel than his knowledge. His knowledge of life and ordinary human beings is so hazy, he really deserves some sort of decoration for it – a medal inscribed 'For Vaguery in the Field'. But it wouldn't do for him to be troubled by any stabs of conscience, however vague. [*Moving down again.*] Besides, he's a patriot and an Englishman, and he doesn't like the idea that he may have been selling out his countryman all these years, so what does he do? The only thing he *can* do – seek sanctuary in his own stupidity. The only way to keep things as much like they always have been as possible, is to make any alternative too much for your poor, tiny brain to grasp. It takes some doing nowadays. It really does. But they knew all about character building at Nigel's school, and he'll make it all right. Don't you worry, he'll make it. And, what's more, he'll do it better than anybody else!

There is no sound, only the plod of Alison's iron. Her eyes are fixed on what she is doing. Cliff stares at the floor. His cheerfulness has deserted him for the moment. Jimmy is rather shakily triumphant. He cannot allow himself to look at either of them to catch their response to his rhetoric, so he moves across to the window, to recover himself, and look out.

(Faber and Faber, 1960, pp. 20–1)

1   *Say in greater detail how the speech embodies a key concept or theme or marks an important moment in the play*

This is Jimmy's first sustained attack on the upper classes. Up to this point he has used his considerable powers of rhetoric to attack various kinds of culture and to taunt both Cliff and Alison into some reaction, but now he releases his full fury on the topic which seems to rile and obsess him most: the attitudes and privileges which he claims to detect in the upper classes. What makes this speech more significant, however, is the fact that it is really an indirect attack on Alison and the values embraced by her family. It is quite shocking in its cruelty to Alison, and from this point onward Jimmy intensifies his venom towards Alison's background and family until he concentrates on Alison herself. Jimmy's attempt to humiliate and wound his wife is embarrassing to Cliff and makes him feel awkward towards his friend Jimmy yet protective towards Alison. Alison's silence and lack of reaction to this speech, shown simply by her plodding ironing and downcast eyes, reveal her suffering and inability to respond to what has obviously been a consistent verbal battering.

2   *Examine the speech characteristics of the character*

Jimmy's style is like that of an orator; his speech is more like a
public address that a speech to two people. It is designed
entirely for effect and he moves around with nervous energy,
flinging out his insults, intending to provoke reactions. His
vocabulary is cleverly chosen, full of witty expressions, puns
and plays upon words, and, above all, is deeply ironic. He uses
rhetorical questions to try to evoke a response, but the whole
speech is really a tirade which cannot be interrupted; it is a
succession of relatively short, powerful sentences which gather
momentum as Jimmy enjoys his verbal invention. He ridicules
his victim by using clichés of patriotism and, clearly, indulges
in some exaggeration for effect. The speech is the product of a
well-educated, extremely literate person, but Jimmy talks *at*
rather than *to* his listeners.

3   *Examine the purpose for which the language is used*

The tone of this speech is ironic and agressive. Jimmy is using
language to achieve the upper hand over a class and set of
attitudes which he despises and which he sees embodied in
Nigel. However, the language is especially an assault on Alison
and he seems anxious to break her down and to be enjoying the
process. The speech doesn't seek an answer; Jimmy is
determined to hold up to ridicule all that 'brother Nigel'
stands for, so that all Alison's roots are destroyed. Language is
being used to taunt and inflict pain but it is also something of a
safety valve for Jimmy, who has nothing but words with which
to fight what he despises. Much of the power of the speech
comes from clever repetition and alliteration.

4   *Say what features of real language are being highlighted*

This is, in some ways, a political speech and has all the
eloquence, passion and cutting edge of a diatribe by a left-wing
reformer. The sentences and phrases have a natural flow, often
in the form of brief statements, and Jimmy builds much of the
speech around the word 'vague'. The reality of the speech
comes from the excitement and vigour with which it is

delivered. We believe in it because Jimmy's character is a mixture of working-class vitality and literary sophistication. The speech is simple in structure and unpretentious in vocabulary; the sentences are designed to be spoken rather than written. The overall effect is of heightened, rhetorical speech.

5   *Read the speech aloud and say how the dramatist makes it effective*

As has been clear throughout this analysis, the speech is one which almost leaps off the page. It builds to a tremendous climax, opening with an almost light-hearted, humorous touch and ending with bitterness. It is punctuated by two sets of stage directions and these create three sections. The first is largely witty but ends with a serious accusation. Jimmy then moves upstage, and when he turns he unleashes a series of insults which culminate in a wicked pun, that Nigel be awarded a medal for 'Vaguery in the Field' – a clever oblique reference to Nigel's military background. The third section brings Jimmy closer to his listeners as he tries to ram home the point that Nigel and his type are affecting all our lives and that the public-school mentality provides a perfect cover for their activities.

One of the most effective features of the speech is its energy and inventiveness. Although there are slight pauses, it seems unbroken in its force and there is a sense in which the speech is much bigger that the situation: it fills the theatre but is overwhelming for the two characters in the small room. Jimmy is like a caged animal, pacing around and delivering his speech with venom and frustration. There is a sharp and effective contrast between the incisiveness and energy of his speech and the vaguery and haziness he is attacking. His speech is also thrown into relief by the impressive Alison, stolidly ironing, and Cliff's uneasy staring at the floor. The stunned silence with which the speech is received unnerves even Jimmy for a moment: all three characters and the audience are aware that this is a more brutal and significant attack than he has launched hitherto, and the wounds are deep. We are left wondering where Jimmy's anger will take him next.

I hope my brief comments on this speech will have reinforced your understanding of the points I have made in this chapter. There are more things which could be said about this key speech, but my remarks should have set you thinking along the right lines. I want to turn now to consider various kinds of play and other means of exploring a playtext.

5

Tackling different kinds of play

ALL the steps that I have suggested so far in your study can be applied to any play, but there comes a stage when you are bound to realise that the particular play you are studying has certain labels and definitions attached to it and that it has characteristics which make it like some other modern plays and unlike others. You may notice this especially if you have come to studying modern drama after having studied Shakespeare, where definitions such as 'tragedy', 'comedy' or 'history' seem fairly watertight and where you have few doubts as to which plays you are talking about if you use these labels. However, you may remember that Polonius in *Hamlet* reels off an extraordinary list of play categories as if to suggest that it is by no means easy to pigeonhole any play: 'tragedy, comedy, history, pastoral, pastoral-comical, historical-pastoral, tragical-historical, tragical-comical-historical-pastoral'. The difficulty of categorising plays particularly applies to modern drama, which belongs to a period of great experimentation and includes works of every imaginable shape and form, lasting anything from thirty seconds to several days.

Nevertheless, despite this variety, modern plays are often grouped into categories and almost certainly you will want and need to become familiar with various terms of reference if you are to discuss the plays in the light of what has been said about them. More important still, you will need to make sure that you are evaluating a play in a manner that is appropriate to its type. We can easily find ourselves asking entirely the wrong questions about a play if we have failed to spot what sort of play it is. It's rather like judging a cricket match as if it were a game of tennis – you end up in the wrong ball game. For example, some modern plays can be maddeningly obscure. In Harold

Pinter's *The Birthday Party* we never discover the true identity of two men who come to a seedy seaside boarding-house and take away a third man; but it's no good writing a criticism of this play as if it were a play by Shaw where a brief biography of each character appears in the text and a satisfactory resolution appears at the end. If Pinter's play *were* like that, it would cease to have the qualities that make it so powerful. Similarly, we cannot evaluate a play by Brecht as if it were by Ibsen.

The next step, then, is to decide what kind of play you have been studying. This may seem a rather late stage at which to make this decision, but it is only now that you have sufficient detail to make an informed decision. Before we look at some possible categories and definitions, you must remember that any one play can fit several categories and that no label is a complete description of any play. Another preliminary is to tackle two terms that have become very widely used in modern-drama study but are very tricky to define: *naturalism* and *realism*. The problem is that the two terms are often used nowadays as if they were synonymous, and, frankly, a great deal of energy can be wasted in trying to find a difference between them. However, the two words had distinct origins as applied to drama, although both came into prominence in the latter half of the nineteenth century.

'Realism' describes a form of drama in which the dramatist shows us people behaving in recognisably human ways in settings which look like the real world we know. Ibsen contributed enormously to the development of realism in the theatre: he discarded 'asides', 'soliloquies' and other non-realistic devices and he was careful to give a purpose to any exposition. Often a character who has just arrived elicits information in what seems a completely natural way, by asking questions. All the scenes have a causal link and lead logically to the *dénouement*, where the threads of the plot are drawn together and a resolution is reached. The characters, costumes, settings and activities are all chosen to reveal important information and are detailed in the stage directions; the characters are also shown to be heavily influenced by heredity and environment and have deep psychological motivation for their behaviour.

Naturalism was a movement in the arts in late-nineteenth-century France. Taking the lead from recent work on evolution and heredity, the naturalists insisted that all man's behaviour was a product of his heredity and environment and that, therefore, he really had no free choice. Art, they said, should reflect this and show man just as he is in his predicament. A naturalistic play must show the characters behaving as people would given the circumstances being shown and there could be no carefully contrived *dénouement* or story-line. Naturalism was to reveal nature as it is: a play should be a 'slice of life' transferred to the stage and must present as much scientific truth as if the characters were being examined under a microscope.

There have probably been no great plays that truly satisfied the definition of naturalism, but many elements of naturalism are present in modern drama and the term is frequently applied to the style of acting that seems appropriate to the dramas of everyday life which form the bulk of the plays written by and since Ibsen. At this point, however, it may be most helpful if we look at some of the broad categories and labels of modern drama.

Well-made plays

The term 'well-made play' is also nineteenth-century in origin and was first used by the playwright Eugène Scribe (1791–1861), whose plays you are unlikely to study! The well-made play has remained a popular formula with modern dramatists because it is a particularly effective means of introducing the sense of the breakdown of an established social order and a complex predicament facing the protagonist. A well-made play consists of three or four acts. A group of people in a lifelike setting are in some way disturbed by the arrival of a new character or some unexpected occurrence; the characters are forced to regroup to bring about a satisfactory end. There is an initial period of careful *exposition* in which the ground is prepared; then a period of *complication*, in which information is withheld, incidents follow in a chain of cause and effect, startling reversals occur and suspense is created, often bringing scenes to a climax; and finally a bringing together of various strands and a resolution of the problems in a *dénouement*. Such writers as Ibsen, Chekhov, Shaw, J. B. Priestley, Joe Orton and

Alan Ayckbourn have all used the formula of the well-made play with great effect because it provides a very satisfying theatrical experience, never allowing the audience to relax completely yet moving towards a resolution that can form a talking-point after the play.

If you have identified the play you are studying as belonging to this type, here are a number of special steps you should add to those you have already carried out.

1   *Discover how the exposition of the play is handled*

As you will recall, the well-made play is invariably realistic and the way in which the audience is provided with background information has to be subtle. In many plays, such as Ibsen's realistic plays, an old friend or a character from the past arrives and there is talk about the intervening years which reveals a lot about the people and their situation. Chekhov's play *The Cherry Orchard* opens with a group of people returning to an old family home, and so there is a period of excited reminiscence which prepares the ground for what is to come. To help yourself determine how the exposition is handled, stop every couple of pages and ask yourself what you now know that you didn't know before, and how you know it.

2   *Discover how each scene is brought to a climax by identifying the events which cause suspense*

These peaks in the action can be represented on a diagram. Try drawing a graph showing where the climaxes occur; this will give you a feel for the shape of the whole play as well as insights into the complications of the plot. As the 'plot thickens', the protagonist's predicament becomes more intense, so this examination of the structure of the play will reinforce your earlier investigations into the nature of this predicament.

3   *Think about the manner and nature of the resolution of the plot in the dénouement*

This will not only bring the story to an end but will resolve the predicament in some way. The resolution may not be happy: it may be death or someone walking out, but it will bring a sense of finality and may involve reconciliation or justice. You should detect how the strands are brought together and how the playwright keeps you in suspense by delaying certain revelations or events. You should also consider what set of ideas are confirmed or challenged by the *dénouement*.

Problem or thesis plays

The description I have offered of a well-made play obviously suits the needs of thrillers, such as the plays of Agatha Christie or Frederick Knott, which are popular with audiences at repertory theatres. However, a more profound form of drama was created out of the apparently straightforward formula of the well-made play by great dramatists such as Ibsen and Shaw. This is the 'problem play', a play which explores a particular social problem, raising many questions about it and provoking the audience into finding answers. Such plays, sometimes known as 'thesis plays' because they mount and work out an argument, may be tragic or comic in essence, but their ideas constitute some issue of deep concern to the dramatist with which he wishes to engage the minds and consciences of the audience. The power of a problem play presented in the well-made format is the contrast between the apparent logical simplicity of the form and the real complexity of the issue with which the play deals. When you are studying such a play you must aim to end up with a grasp of both, so after your initial analysis of the play apply the following steps:

1   *Define all the factors which motivate the characters or in some way affect their behaviour* (these may include environment, heredity, personal characteristics, ambitions, attitudes and moral codes)

2   *Identify what decisions have to be made by the main characters and what moral/social issues are involved*

3   *Try to detect the dramatist's stance towards his topic and state clearly in your notes where you feel he leaves the matter open-ended*

Audiences have quite frequently been shocked by problem plays: Ibsen's *A Doll's House* and *Ghosts* were greeted with howls of protest. Someone described *Ghosts* as 'an open sewer' and a press review called it 'a dirty deed done in public'. In the same way, television audiences in the late 1960s were so disturbed by the play *Cathy Come Home* that it led to the formation of the organisation Shelter to care for the homeless. Thus we can see that in order fully to understand a problem play we need to understand the problem, so a final step is

4   *Discover all you can about social conditions and moral attitudes pertaining at the time the play was written*

Some authors (such as Shaw) provide a preface to their plays explaining some of the issues with which they deal, and many play editors include a good, scholarly introduction that is useful in the same way. Editors will often include some evidence from other contemporary sources to illustrate why a particular issue was of especial interest to the dramatist. So, for example, you will be in a far better position to study Ibsen's *A Doll's House* if you know about nineteenth-century attitudes towards marriage. There are plenty of problem plays still being written as dramatists continue to attack society's laws, attitudes and injustices, and you would do well to acquaint yourself with plays by such writers as Barry Keefe and Caryl Churchill.

The new realism

Like all formulas, there *is* something predictable about the well-made play, and many playwrights anxious to make their distinctive voices heard have found it restricting and outmoded. Since the Second World War the most innovative and interesting dramatists have abandoned the form and experimented with alternatives. This is largely because, although the well-made play as refined by Ibsen or Shaw was intended to convey reality, in the hands of lesser imitators it had come to seem contrived and artificial. Writers such as Arthur Miller, John Osborne and Arnold Wesker were anxious to present aspects of the reality of everyday existence in new and striking ways. Their settings were equally realistic but sometimes showed a squalor or ordinariness unfamiliar to theatre audiences. Instead of elegant drawing-rooms with drinks from cocktail cabinets, there were dingy tenements, bedsits and poorly furnished small houses, with drinks straight from the fridge. Instead of articulate and elegant conversation, there was language full of vigour from the working-class tradition. Such plays usually show people struggling against the pressures which society puts on them, so, once you have concluded studying the play through the steps I have outlined so far,

1 *Sum up why you think it was necessary for the dramatist to show social reality with such detail*

You might like to take these opening moments from scene 4 of Arnold Wesker's **Chips with Everything**, a play about young men doing their National Service (compulsory military service) in the Royal Air Force:

> *Sound of marching feet. Marching stops. The lecture hall.*
> *Boys enter and sit on seats. Enter the* WING COMMANDER, *boys rise.*

> WING COMMANDER. Sit down, please. I'm your Wing Commander. You think we are at peace. Not true. We are never at peace. The human being is in a constant state of war and we must be prepared, each against the other. History has taught us this and we must learn. The reasons why and wherefore are not our concern. We are simply the men who must be prepared. You, why do you look at me like that?
> PIP. I'm paying attention, sir.
> WING COMMANDER. There's insolence in those eyes, lad – I recognize insolence in a man; take that glint out of your eyes, your posh tones don't fool me. We are simply the men who must be prepared. Already the aggressors have a force far superior to ours. Our efforts must be intensified. We need a fighting force and it is for this reason you are being trained here, according to the best traditions of the RAF. We want you to be proud of your part, unashamed of the uniform you wear. But you must not grumble too much if you find that government facilities for you, personally, are not up to standard. We haven't the money to spare. A Meteor, fully armed, is more important than a library. The CO of this camp is called Group Captain Watson. His task is to check any tendency in his officers to practical jokes, to discountenance any disposition in his officers to gamble or indulge in extravagant expenditure; to endeavour, by example and timely intervention, to promote a good understanding and prevent disputes. Group Captain Watson is a busy man, you will rarely see him. You, why are you smiling?
> SMILER. I'm not sir, it's natural, I was born like it.

WING COMMANDER. Because I want this taken seriously, you know, from all of you. Any questions?

WILFE. Sir, if the aggressors are better off than us, what are they waiting for?

WING COMMANDER. What's your name?

WILFE. 247 Seaford, sir.

WING COMMANDER. Any other questions?

Exit. Enter SQUADRON LEADER. *The boys rise*

(*New English Dramatists 7*, Penguin, 1965, pp. 25–6)

Even after this short incident we can see exactly what conditions are like for the young recruits. Throughout the play it is the vivid portrayal of these conditions which engages our interest. In a series of short scenes we are given an alarming montage of life in the armed forces; the awful conditions and attitudes produce casualties and survival techniques and at the end nothing has changed except the lives of the young men who are forced to go through what is shown as a dehumanising process. The audience in a play such as this is constantly jolted into realising that the dramatist has something disturbing to say about some aspect of life that goes on all the time.

2 Ask why the playwright has chosen not to write just a traditional well-made play

This may seem a rather negative thing to be asked to consider but I think we all probably feel that the well-made play is a comfortable form with which we can cope easily and that any deviation from it has the sense of the unexpected about it.

3 Ask if the play is some form of protest

During the 1950s and 1960s, British plays which showed a realistic picture of life, in what were often fairly squalid conditions, were nicknamed 'kitchen-sink' dramas and a similar label was given to some painters of the period. This somewhat dismissive description overlooked the fact that such plays were often written as a protest against the drabness and injustice of life. You should be able to detect the playwright's standpoint and understand the means whereby he confronts the audience with the reality of other people's lives. Not all plays which are set in rather drab, everyday surroundings are a protest – on the contrary, many show the warmth and vitality which exist in the most unpromising conditions. In recent years, however, the kind of realism of the kitchen-sink drama has been taken up more successfully by television. You should not, however, confuse the entertainment offered over a prolonged period by the 'everyday' dramas of a soap opera with the intensive experience of seeing a play in a theatre. Soap operas are just as cunningly constructed as a well-made play, each episode being carefully brought to a climax to ensure that you want to watch the next. 'Real life', as we well know, does not consist of a series of well-ordered scenes – it would be much easier if it did; many people's lives are singularly uneventful and at times boring, so if a dramatist aims to show real life he must show all this too. You must decide how a playwright has *created* and *sustained* interest in his characters and their situations, however mundane they may be. In another play by Arnold Wesker, *Roots*, we see a picture of the humdrum and monotonous lives of a family in rural Norfolk. For them the passing of a bus is an event, as it is also for two old ladies in Pinter's *Black and White*. Yet, although the audience must *sense* the characters' boredom, they themselves must not be bored. This is a problem for you to tackle as you examine the play more closely.

Similarly, you will need to confront the problem of continuing relevance. *Chips with Everything* is a good example of this problem: the play is about men doing their National Service in Britain in the 1940s and 1950s. To this extent the play is no longer of immediate relevance, as nobody is forced to do National Service in Britain now. All the carefully shown details might be thought to be as merely of historic interest. But beneath the surface reality of events and conditions there is the whole question of human nature into which Wesker delves, and the military mind is by no means extinct. We might therefore feel that the play has ceased to be a protest against a specific set of conditions and has become more universal in its application. When you study a play you must be careful not to judge its meaning and value solely in relation to a set of social conditions that operated when it was written, although you should certainly be aware of these conditions. Plays of so-called 'social realism' often raise much wider issues, which guarantees them what Dr Jonathan Miller has very aptly described as an 'after life'.

Very often you will end up asking yourself 'How real is real?' and that is a very good question to ask. The playwright simulates just as much reality as suits his purpose; indeed, you should now realise that any relation between what happens on a stage and the real world that is being represented all depends on the way in which an audience's perception is manipulated. Once you get the general feeling from your reading of the play that it could be described in some senses as 'realistic', take a careful look again at the following features.

(a) *Structure*. Structure is how a play is put together. Quickly look to see how many acts, scenes or episodes the play is divided into and how they are *related*. You may find modern plays which seem like well-made plays, or by contrast a whole series of short scenes which are more like the rapidly changing shots of a film. They may follow sequentially in time or may appear to flash back and forward; they may all take place in one or a few places or range over many differing locations. What concerns you at this point is how the writer reinforces the sense of reality through the structure of the play. It may be that a series of loosely connected scenes provides a feeling of real life by enabling the audience to build up a complete picture in their imaginations; on the other hand, the sense of truth to real life may be achieved by a deliberate avoidance of climaxes to scenes or of a neat pattern of beginning, middle and end – rather as if the dramatist has taken a random 'slice of life'.

(b) *Setting*. Look at the details of the setting and the way that the playwright creates the illusion of reality. You may find exhaustive descriptions of rooms, furniture and exteriors and there may be indications of the ways in which the playwright wants the scene to be built on stage. In *Death of a Salesman*, which is in *some* respects a realistic play, Arthur Miller indicates how the audience will watch scenes in bedrooms and kitchen from the same viewpoint. This involves some contrivance on the part of the scene-designer, and what is to be constructed is a series of levels with cut-away walls. However, within each space there is careful realism. The majority of modern plays are set indoors and you should pay particular attention to the environment which people create for themselves and which affects them. A junk-filled room, a kitchen or a comfortable lounge (for example) makes a statement which you must interpret. Notice how the playwright builds the environment: you will find it helpful to look at the stage directions of Strindberg's play *Miss Julie*, which offers a very early example of this kind of realism.

(c) *Situation*. If you feel that what the playwright presents is a 'real' situation, try to define and summarise what you mean. You will probably be talking about something which is in some ways familiar and which you can explain in logical terms. You will be able to say why the people are where they are, why they behave as they do and what the consequences of their actions will be. If you are able to imagine that you are witnessing the goings-on in someone else's life, then you will know that a kind of reality has been achieved. Why, you must ask yourself, is this of *interest* to you? Many modern plays show characters trapped by their situation. These characters are usually 'ordinary' people with whom we can identify, and the dramatic interest lies in their response to their predicament.

(d) *Dialogue*. You will have considered the language of the play in some detail by this time, but think again how this relates to the idea that these are real people talking. Much of the language of 'well-made' plays in the first half of this century was elegant and witty but represented the real conversation of a small minority of the population. More recent plays have sought to utilise the language patterns of much larger sections of the population, but this is never a static affair: regional characteristics, racial differences, 'imported' vocabulary and new jargon all change what we would recognise as 'real' language, so you must look carefully at the play to see how the playwright has created a kind of speech that seems up-to-date yet will not necessarily seem out-dated in a few years. You will find expressions and phrases which relate quite definitely to a certain period – identify these and notice how they give authenticity to the action.

The theatre of the absurd

Suppose you are asked to read Harold Pinter's short play *The Dumb Waiter*. Two men, Ben and Gus, sit on two beds in a dingy room. One reads out extracts from a newspaper; the other takes off his shoe and discovers it contains a cigarette packet. They talk in a desultory fashion, debating at some length whether you should say 'light the gas', 'put on the kettle' or 'light the kettle', and revealing that they are hired assassins. Where, precisely, they are, who the victim is and why, suddenly, a 'dumb waiter' crashes down into the room from a supposedly empty upstairs are only a few of the mass of questions which remain more or less unanswered at the end of the play. In one sense the conversation of the two men seems real, yet it gets nowhere; the characters seem real, yet we know no more about them at the end of the play than we did at the beginning. In short, you simply cannot *explain* the play and it presents a view of life that seems chaotic and meaningless.

Such a description would fit all the plays of Samuel Beckett, one of the most influential of all modern dramatists, and, to a lesser extent, those of Pinter. The phenomenon of the so-called 'theatre of the absurd', which had its origins in the 1950s, presents particular difficulties for students because the plays are both inaccessible on the page and frequently baffling on the stage. There are times when reading a good problem play can be almost as satisfying as reading a good novel, but this is certainly not true of 'absurd' drama. The first thing to grasp is that such plays work by presenting a series of images in the theatre. They are conceived as something which the audience must experience even though they may not be able to offer a logical explanation of the details of that experience. Beckett, for example, offers us images of human beings in varying states of decay: characters in dustbins; characters almost buried in earth; a huge mouth occupying the stage; and so on. Time scales are various, with one play (*Breath*) just thirty seconds long; sounds and silence are organised without reference to the normal patterns of 'everyday' life. These are all powerful images which only have significance if you see and hear them. So, if you cannot get to see a performance of any play you are studying, either organise one yourself or, as a poor substitute, try to imagine it vividly, in performance. Picture what the actors actually *do* and how they say the words.

Secondly, be honest about what baffles or disturbs you in the play. You will be nearer to appreciating it than you think, because such reactions are probably just what the playwright intended. Don't expect explanations – there won't be any, except that you will begin to get the feeling of what the play is about in a broader sense. You may, for example, never be able to explain why, in what is supposedly a disused restaurant, a dumb waiter suddenly descends bringing messages from outside; yet, as a powerful image of the obscure menace which threatens us from outside and which may be a different fear for every one of us, the dumb waiter is potent and appropriate. You will find the language unnerving if it seems to get nowhere, but, again, be honest with your appraisal of it; observe its patterns and clichés and you will find an uncanny resemblance to 'real' speech – indeed, you may find a greater reality in its seemingly disorganised and pointless qualities. Don't allow your expectations that a play should tell a story or 'make sense' to stand in the way of your attitudes.

Thirdly, consider all the ways in which the play frustrates your expectations. The chances are that there will be elements of realism: the setting may be detailed and domestic and the talk may be like ordinary conversation – so you may think, 'Ah, we have a realistic play which will pose a problem which will be eventually resolved', only to be utterly frustrated. Or there may be bizarre elements which prevent your making sense of what you see. In two of Ionesco's plays, for example, the whole stage fills with furniture until in one play the two characters on stage have conversations with people whom they *imagine* to be sitting in the dozens of chairs and in the other the actors vanish beneath the furniture. Normally we expect stage furniture to signify that we are looking at a domestic situation and we even deduce information about the status and wealth of the characters from the environment they have created for themselves. But in Ionesco's plays furniture seems to serve a different purpose and deductions become impossible. You may be equally frustrated by a lack of plot, structure or information about the characters. If you find yourself thinking 'This is not how a play should be', then you are revealing that you have certain expectations. You may well share these with many theatre-goers, and the playwright has calculatingly played upon this fact. Notice how the dramatist has worked on traditional theatre forms and reversed some of the processes.

Finally, consider the kind of reality that the playwright *has* created. He presents a particular view of the world through a series of images which may remain imprecise. Reflect on the absurdity of some aspects of our lives and consider how the playwright has conveyed this sense of the lack of order.

What does it all mean?

Students often make the mistake of thinking that the meaning of a play is there, embedded in the text, simply waiting for them to dig it out. Both Beckett and Pinter have always been quite adamant that they are under no obligation to come on at the end of a play and explain the meaning: meanings are created in the minds of the audience both during and after a performance – the text only becomes a play when the audience give meaning to what they see and hear. Indeed, 'What does this play mean?' is really the wrong question to ask. When asked what his plays were *about*, Harold Pinter once replied, 'The weasel under the cocktail cabinet', which is a striking metaphor for the fears, guilt, aggression, insecurity and fantasies which operate beneath the surface of our lives and are so vividly portrayed in his plays.

Epic theatre

Along with Beckett, the German playwright Bertolt Brecht has been one of the strongest influences on the modern theatre. The problem with Brecht is that students study not only his plays but also his various, much publicised, theories about drama, and then find it difficult to relate the two. Brecht was both playwright and director and many of his plays evolved during rehearsal. Naturally, Brecht had strong ideas as to how his plays should be performed, but he also had deeply felt convictions about the theatre in general, and all these opinions have been preserved in his many writings. Students often, quite understandably, forget that Brecht wrote as a result of his wide experience, and that he was not prescribing so much as arguing and reflecting; so, although he may have advocated certain styles of performance and certain aims, this may not be immediately apparent from reading his plays. I have known students be very worried and feel very inadequate because they couldn't honestly say that they could detect Brecht's famous 'alienation' effect in a play they were reading.

Before you begin looking for Brechtian characteristics in a play you are studying, it might help you to know precisely why Brecht's plays had such an impact in the British theatre. Brecht's work was first seen in Britain in the 1950s, when the Berliner Ensemble, Brecht's own company, brought their production of *Mother Courage* to London. The idea of an acting 'ensemble' was itself revolutionary; it was a group of actors who regularly worked together, devising the plays with the playwright and rehearsing in an experimental fashion. There were no 'stars' and the democratic group had become committed to a particularly economic style. There was no attempt to deceive the audience into believing that they were not in a theatre: there was no curtain to rise revealing a realistic interior; spotlights were unmasked, and no effort was made to conceal scene changes. The actors, using detailed and realistic props, behaved as if they were telling a story, at one level deeply involved, at another able to stand back from the story and comment upon it. The play itself was a series of short scenes each introduced by a projected headline saying what it was about. The setting was the Thirty Years War in Europe, and, although there was no plot as such, the events portrayed centred on things which happened to Mother Courage, an anti-heroine who hauled a canteen wagon, trading with rival armies and scheming her way to survival by even allowing her children to die. The action was punctuated by songs in the style of Berliner café songs, and the total effect was to show ordinary, fallible people caught up in a futile war with no control over events and confronted by difficult choices.

What I have tried to describe is a piece of 'epic theatre', and if you visit the theatre regularly you will recognise that many of its characteristics have become common practice. Brecht developed this style in order that audiences should not become so involved in the story-line and lives of the characters that they were unable to reflect on the issues with which the play was concerned. He constantly insisted that he wanted his audience to be more like the spectators at a boxing-match – enjoying the skill of the boxers and the contest itself but also able to argue about the outcome. He wanted to confront the audience with a problem and challenge them to think of a solution. Because he wanted plays to serve this didactic purpose, he often called them 'parables' or 'teaching pieces', and because he was a Marxist he insisted that change is possible if people set their minds to it.

Brecht's anti-heroes are often confronted with difficult choices, so the protagonist's predicament is relatively easy to define, but students are often over-serious in their approach to the plays; the plays do deal with very serious issues but you should get a sense of their rich entertainment value too. The additional steps I have suggested when looking at various 'realistic' plays will help you with epic plays, but you might also think of them under the following headings:

(a) *Structure*. Examine the choice of episodes. They will not usually be causally related, so discover in what sense they *are* related. Note the total time scale of the play and any linking-device, such as a story-teller, narrator or headlines, that the playwright uses. Pay particular attention to the positioning of the songs – don't skip over these but try to hear an original musical setting of them. Decide on the effect which a song directed straight at the audience will have. How does a song in a Brechtian play differ from a song in a romantic 'musical'?

(b) *Staging*. Plays by Brecht and those who have used some of his techniques often appear to demand elaborate scenery, but in fact they are designed to be staged with great economy. Notice how locations – interiors, exteriors and combinations of these – can be represented simply, often by no more than a central property such as a table, cart or bar on an otherwise bare stage. Such properties, along with film and slide projections and on-stage musicians, play a vital part in transforming the stage space so that it represents something concrete in the minds of the audience. Think how different this approach is from the realism of Ibsen, Strindberg or Shaw, where the room itself almost seems to be a character in the play. If you think through this difference you will see how it extends to the performance style. In Ibsen, or any other 'realistic' playwright, it would be unacceptable for an actor to step out of role in the carefully constructed room and talk to the audience, but in a piece of epic theatre there is a two-way traffic between stage and auditorium – rather like in a music hall. British audiences have never quite responded to Brecht's plays in the way that, for example, the East Germans do: in East Germany you can find theatres packed with people, including soldiers, laughing and applauding at his plays. In Britain, the problem is partly that it is only recently that workable translations of what are often wonderfully poetic and witty plays have become available, but it is also that productions of Brecht tend to be approached with a deep seriousness which suffocates them.

(c) *Situation*. Epic theatre poses social and moral problems for the audience to consider. Once you have identified the dilemmas facing the hero or anti-hero, decide what social or moral issues these raise. Often a character is faced with a difficult choice, so you must consider the basis for condemning or approving the choice that makes the character and try to understand the consequences. You also need to have a very clear idea of the pressures which a particular situation creates. Brecht's most famous plays deal with events which are far removed from us both in time and place, so you must determine what gives them relevance to a modern audience.

What if the play I'm studying fits none of the categories?

The first thing to remember is that no playwright ever set out to acquire a label and that, although he or she may have been influenced by broader movements in the theatre and the arts, every playwright has an individual voice. We have looked at the main trends in modern drama, but inevitably there are plays which do not belong to any one of these but appear to have characteristics of several. It is sometimes helpful to group playwrights to discuss common issues and trends: there are, for example, excellent books on realism or the absurd and, obviously, you need to know if the plays you are studying are likely to be mentioned. But a lable is only an indicator, and the playwright certainly hasn't failed if a label refuses to stick! Many of the modern movements in art, such as naturalism, dadaism, surrealism and expressionism, contain elements that can be identified in plays, and, like the other movements we have discussed, these provide certain terms of reference to describe features of the writing. However, *all* plays have some form of structure, setting and dialogue and it is these which you should study. You will then discover which, if any, of the labels are helpful in describing and accounting for what you have found. If you think a particular label does fit, you must be able to demonstrate why: there is no point in using such terms unless you have grasped their meaning and can show you have. If the play you are studying belongs to no obvious category, don't worry: many plays are like this. However, you will find some knowledge of the main trends in modern drama a useful tool in coming to grips with the nature and purpose of modern plays.

Symbolism

In the next chapter, which suggests some practical exercises, I introduce the idea that every action on stage is a sign and every object a symbol. A symbol is something which stands for something else; so, for example, the tape-recorder which we see on stage in *Death of a Salesman* (probably acquired by the 'props' department with some difficulty) stands for the tape-recorder in Howard Wagner's office. But it stands for much more than that: it is the latest gadget acquired by a consumer society which is rapidly devaluing human life; it is the new object of attention which prevents Howard, the boss, from giving proper attention to his employee Willy Loman. The recorder symbolises everything that makes the ruthless materialism of the play so ugly. In Ibsen's plays the qualify of the light is often symbolic: sometimes, like truth, it is too bright to bear and at other times it is murky like the characters' motives. It's easy both to over-simplify and over-complicate symbolism, but you should think carefully about the effects and objects with which the playwright has filled the play and see how they relate to the themes and issues which you have identified.

Exploring a play

Students often get depressed because they feel that *they* cannot find in a play all that teachers, critics and other students claim to have noticed. You may have felt this as you have followed some of the suggestions in this book, but you must remember not to expect everything to come to you at once. The more you acquaint yourself with a play by reading, workshop activities or theatre visits, the more you need to *think* about the play for ideas to settle in your mind. No good play is going to yield up all its qualities immediately; the very fact that it amuses, interests, baffles or angers you should mean that it lingers in the mind, and things will occur to you long after you have closed the book or left the theatre. Sometimes a chance remark or a piece of criticism will illuminate something that puzzled you weeks ago. This, of course, is hardly much comfort in the high pressure of examination-based study, but it is a good reason for distrusting some of your initial responses and for giving yourself time to return to a play after a short lapse. Don't be afraid, either, to change your mind if, after a period of thought, or a visit to the theatre, you begin to see things differently. Indeed, it might be a good idea if I now say something specifically about the experience of seeing a play on the stage.

Making sense of a theatre visit

I am going to assume that you have worked your way systematically through this book and that you now have the opportunity to see one of the plays you have been studying performed in a theatre. If, however, you have been skimming through the book and have decided to read this section, I want to say some things which should be useful to you as well. The importance of theatre-going cannot be over-emphasised. If you want to study modern drama you should take every opportunity to see plays in production, whether or not they are the particular set plays which you must eventually answer questions about. You need to familiarise yourself with the conventions of theatre and you cannot really hope to do this if your experience of theatre is restricted to a couple of compulsory visits. Furthermore, you have to get used to the idea that the purpose of a theatre visit as part of the process of studying a play can easily become blurred if you get bogged down in a discussion of whether the production was good or bad. I have often known worthy parties of students and their teachers expend a lot of energy on an assessment of the merits of a particular production when it is quite obvious that their approach has done little or nothing to further their understanding of the play. Certainly a consideration of how actors and actresses interpret a playwright's intentions is part of the process of drama study, but very often reactions to a production are a result of the gap between the imagined performance which students have developed in their minds and the actual performance which they witness taking place in front of them.

A visit to any production, however 'good' or 'bad', can be instructive, and for this reason I am going to imagine that you are visiting a professional touring production of Harold Pinter's **The Birthday Party** that has come to your local theatre. I shall guide you through the first few minutes. The first thing you notice when you take your seat is that the stage is an open, thrust stage which projects into the auditorium and that there are no curtains. As you look around you see the various spotlights hung ready to light the stage and you may reflect on the kind of influence that Brecht has had on modern theatre – there is no attempt to disguise the fact that you are in a theatre. Positioned in the centre of the stage area is the set – there is a rather dingy room furnished with solid but drab furniture and decorated with fading wallpaper and tasteless ornaments. A staircase leads into the room on one side, above it an archway of moulded plaster and beside it a door, over which there is a glass panel with a house name on it which you can see written back to front because it is intended to be read from outside. On the other side of the room is another door and a serving-hatch, both of which lead to a kitchen in which there is a real kitchen sink. You may not have thought of the play as a 'kitchen sink' drama, but there is the sink. All this detail is actually conveyed by one long wall which runs at a slight angle across the rear of the stage and two very short walls which are attached at either end and project forwards towards the auditorium. These two short walls are actually cut away as though someone has taken a pair of scissors and randomly trimmed them, and the edges seem to fade into the black background of the stage. The 'floor' area is designated by a carpet, but even this is cut off, because its front edge merges into the front edge of the stage; and, although a single light bulb hangs in the middle of the 'room', there is actually no ceiling and the upper boundaries merge into darkness.

How easily you accept this highly artificial contrivance as 'realistic'! There are enough real and familiar objects for this setting to represent a room in a run-down boarding house, and, although some of the details may differ from what you were expecting, the characters who you know will walk through the door will fit perfectly into this environment created by the stage-designer and all the events of the play will 'work' in this setting. There is the packet of cornflakes, the breakfast table, the tatty mixture of chairs and so on.

The sense of reality leads you to believe that the play will provide clear explanations, for, as the philosopher Ryan put it, 'what we look for is that information which, when appropriately put together, yields us an argument to the effect that the event in question was what we should rationally expect'. You know that this idea, which will dominate the attitude of the audience, will, in the case of this play, be upset. Rational explanations are likely to be lacking, but, whereas a play with surrealist scenery may lead us to expect them to be missing, the recognisable interior with its staircase and kitchen makes the audience think otherwise.

All this is available for you to observe before the play beings, and it is important that you take the trouble: as you do so, you are already thinking about the decisions made, reflecting on the degree of realism and the stage conventions adopted by the director. You *could* waste your time at this point, but once the action starts you won't get so good a chance to think so constructively about staging.

When the house lights dim there is a brief total darkness before the stage lights come up to reveal Meg, the landlady, already in her kitchen banging about with crockery and saucepans and turning on the tap to fill a kettle. Again, you accept without question that the rooms *are* lit by the light bulbs you see hanging and which are turned on by the brass switch you see by the door, but *in fact* a couple of dozen spotlights are focused on the stage area. As Meg, a woman in her late fifties you think, continues with what seem like breakfast preparations, her husband Petey enters. He wears a brown overall, a peaked cap and a ticket machine. You know he is a deckchair attendant if you have read the play; if you haven't, that fact, and the fact that Petey and Meg are married, are established through the dialogue quite early on. Petey slowly removes his cap, overall and ticket machine, hangs them up, takes a cardigan, puts it on, sits at the table, opens a newspaper and begins to eat his cornflakes. Meg calls out, 'Is that you?' and there follows a desultory conversation through the serving-hatch about cornflakes and fried bread. A little later they talk about the contents of the newspaper – you observe the simple, repetitive patterns of their dialogue which look so flat on the page but which now sound so real, so inconsequential and so funny. In spite of the fact that there are no jokes, no comic business and no obviously farcical situations, the audience are laughing almost from the first spoken word. You notice, also, the long and quite frequent silences, the fact that no *story* as such appears to be unfolding in the dialogue, and the extraordinary sense that these two people are going through a ritual in which they consciously avoid real communication. In one sense it seems meaningless, yet it does establish a cosy social order: this sense of social order is enhanced by the references to Stanley, who is not yet up and therefore not on stage – a pattern which Pinter exploits to the full in the dialogue. You notice, therefore, when this social order is threatened: when Petey mentions that two men came up to him on the beach and enquired about staying at the boarding-house, the simple scene of *exposition*, which gives some indication of what the general situation is, moves into the first phase of *complication*. You sense this in the theatre through the tension which the mention of the two men produces in Meg and later in Stanley, the only guest currently staying with her. You will also be aware how the conversations among the five characters in the play have their own distinctive rhythms depending on who is present.

None of this observation prevents you from enjoying the performance or being affected by it. You will be aware of the effect which the performance is having on the audience. As each character enters you will quickly readjust your mental picture of him or her to accord with the new image of the character presented by the actor or actress. Meg may look younger than you had imagined her, Stanley older; Lulu may be a Cockney, although you had pictured her coming from Birmingham. As you watch the play you are struck by how little the characters reveal about themselves. When Stanley, who has once been a pianist on the pier, gives an account of a concert he gave in Lower Edmonton, you begin to doubt the truth of it and you realise that the text of the play appears to be almost like the sub-text. The most disturbing things to witness are the games which the characters play – at first apparently harmless, as with the games between Meg and Stanley, but then increasingly sinister and deadly. Suddenly watching a game or a ritual is totally different from imagining it, and the moments when the characters and the audience are plunged into darkness are chilling.

Your experience in the theatre is a mixture of analysis and emotional involvement. You now have a chance to see the practical implications of what you have studied in private. *The Birthday Party* may not be a play you are studying, but you can learn from the deductions you might make from seeing it. A visit to see a play by Stoppard or Miller might present different details, but your reflections on what you see or hear would need to be similar. You see the protagonist struggling with the predicament, you see the effect on people of the breakdown of social order, and your ear detects the features of dialogue you have studied. There is enormous pleasure in hearing what you have identified as key speeches performed, and you may feel the need to rethink aspects of their meaning – notice the concrete decisions made about inflections, emphasis or pause in speeches you know well; another 'reading' adds to your fund of experience and terms of reference. Notice, also, how the designer has interpreted or adapted the scenic requirements, how the director has located the action in a precise historical period, and how the audience react to what they see. For a student, all this is more important than whether you thought the performance was 'good', because you should have far wider terms of reference than such a comment implies – any live performance can reinforce your study of the play and give you a far clearer idea of what you mean when you come to write about it in an essay or examination question. And that includes your own performance of the play or your own 'practical' work on it, something I deal with in the next chapter.

6

Practical workshops and drama study

A DRAMA 'workshop' is rather like a science laboratory in which experiments are carried out and ideas tested. However much we may remind ourselves that a play as a work of art only really exists in performance, it is difficult to put that belief into practice when we are studying. The workshop approach to the study of a text provides an opportunity for us to come to grips with some of the implications of knowing that the printed page is a blueprint for action on a stage. The term 'workshop' is a relatively recent description of a particular approach to drama and was popularised in Britain by the director Joan Littlewood, working in the tradition of the great German playwright and director Bertold Brecht. It has come to mean an experimental approach in which actors engage in join exploration of a play rather than follow the precise instructions of a director, but it also implies a simple space with none of the elaborate trappings of commercial theatre.

The suggestions in this chapter assume that you have access to an uncluttered but fairly small space in which you can work with other members of a class or tutorial group. It is perfectly possible, however, to carry out some of these ideas at home with one other person and even, if you have no alternative, on your own. The whole prospect of a 'drama workshop' may of course horrify you; you may think that it's only for people who are 'good at acting' or like showing off; you may feel very inhibited (in spite of the fact that modern students are supposedly uninhibited!) or you may simply have never had any experience of this kind of thing before. Give yourself and this approach a chance. Read the entire chapter before you rebel against it, and discuss it with other students and teachers. I am assuming *no* previous experience on your part and no particular talent for acting: but I am assuming that you are a serious student who actually wants to understand a play from all possible angles.

If you are to understand how a play works, it is important for you to grasp that the person who wrote it understood how the theatre works from the inside. All the modern dramatists who have achieved a degree of permanent success have been involved in the theatre, either as actors, as directors or as close associate of directors. They have often allowed their work to be shaped in rehearsal, have held firm views on acting-styles and have known how actors work. They have often been in rebellion against the performance modes of their day and have sometimes had a particular performer in mind for a part when they wrote it. These are all good reasons for you to explore the text in practical situations, and this will help you in the most difficult aspect of drama study: concrete decisions. Take, for example, the way in which a character speaks a certain line and another character reacts to it. In the privacy of your own room and read silently to yourself, that line could be 'spoken' in any one of a hundred ways – you need never reach a final decision and you can leave the precise meaning 'open'. Once you have to speak that line or hear someone else speak it in a workshop reading of a scene, a decision has to be made about precisely how that line should sound. You may *then* decide that the first decision was wrong and in the experimental atmosphere of the workshop you can move towards a satisfactory decision. Once you try out a line in context, so many factors suddenly come into focus. Perhaps the character has just run up stairs, been on her feet all day, found himself in a dark room – all such factors will affect the speaking of every word. The way in which one character elects to deliver one line will, in turn, affect another character's reaction to it, and you can only really *react* as a character when you've listened to what has been said to you.

None of this will demand great acting-skill on your part, but it will demand concentration, imagination and a willingness to change your mind. Most modern plays are suitable for study in this way, because there are rarely more than a few characters on stage at a time and all the suggestions which follow can be applied to *any* play you are studying. The basis of many drama workshop situations is improvisation: that is, acting which does not arise directly from speaking a text. Many students are now acquiring experience in improvisation and appreciating its significance, but don't be daunted by this: if you are interested in any aspect of living you will find you can improvise – after all, that is what most of us do most of the time, isn't it?

Some basic concepts

The first activities are designed to help you explore the idea of theatre in a rudimentary way and to focus your attention on the conventions of performance. You will find that I constantly ask questions of you but provide few answers. Knowing how to ask the right questions is one of the essentials of studying modern drama.

(a) *A stage*. Clear a space in the middle of the room and decide that this is the area in which action will take place. Define the area carefully: this is your 'stage'; anywhere outside it is not. Now place an object of furniture in the space. At once this has significance – it is no longer just a chair or whatever; it stands for something else – maybe a chair in Willy Loman's house, maybe a throne. If you are able to focus a spotlight on it, it becomes even more significant, because the attention of the spectators is drawn towards it. You can add other items to the stage: you may be able to introduce a change of level in the form of a rostrum or set of steps; you may add small items such as books or newspapers. Anything in the empty space we call the stage is a *symbol* – it stands for more than itself. Now select the opening scenes of two modern plays and decide how you might present them on the stage you have defined. Notice how easily the space can be transformed to represent anywhere you wish and how simply such features as the edge of a room or the presence of a window may be indicated.

(b) *Further transformation*. Still using your space in the middle of the room, create areas which indicate at least two rooms. If you have some simple stage lighting available, use it to help define the rooms and the moments when action switches from one to the other. Remember where an audience might be able to sit in this instance: if the 'stage' is in the centre we have built a 'theatre-in-the-round', which means that the audience will sit on all four sides of the stage and that we are using 'arena' staging. This in turn means that, although we give *indications* of such things as doors, windows and walls, much is left to the audience's imagination. This is one of the main conventions of performance: the audience agrees that in order to view the play it must flesh out many of the details in its imagination.

(c) *An actor.* Either return to your bare space or use the stage you have created. Ask one of your group to sit in the space. What questions does this raise? The moment an actor enters the stage space we have the ingredients for drama: we wonder where he comes from, who he is, where he is going, what he is going to do and, above all, what is the significance of his actions and activities. Ask your 'actor' to move around and do various things of his choice – everything becomes a *sign*, telling us something about the actor and his situation: suggest to the actor that he should sit perfectly still but look around or stare in one direction – discuss the effect this creates. If you catch a glimpse of a member of the 'audience' moving or looking around, it has very little significance for you; but the moment an actor on stage does anything or does *not* do anything this is some kind of sign – at once you start to question further.

(d) *A scene.* Probably the first, unconscious question which members of an audience ask when they see actors on stage representing characters in a play is 'What are they doing there?' Generally speaking, playwrights answer the question pretty quickly, so that within a few minutes of a play's starting the audience knows in general terms what is going on. In pairs now devise a short scene in which it is perfectly obvious within two minutes where the characters are and why they are there. When your group has watched all the scenes (which should be presented on your 'arena stage') discuss the techniques used by the 'actors' to put across the vital information.

Now, in the same pairs, devise two-minute scenes in which by the conclusion of the scene your audience is no nearer to knowing where you are and what is going on – this, by the way, is much more difficult! Again discuss how the effect is achieved. As a next stage take the following scenes and present them:

1   A single actor is sitting looking up at a bucket which hangs from the roof in a junk-filled room. There is the sound of

water dripping into the bucket. A door slams off-stage and there is the sound of voices. The actor stands and leaves the room.

2 The empty stage simply contains a tree, possibly represented by a hat-stand or similar object. Two scruffy-looking people sit beneath it and for two minutes discuss what time it is, but fail to agree.

3 A woman in bed upstairs hears her husband come in the front door. He is a tired travelling salesman; she calls out to him and he comes into the bedroom and says what a dreadful day he has had.

Remember that you must find a way of conveying every piece of information I have given you, but no more. Discuss the differences between the scenes, which are loosely based on three modern plays. In what sense do scenes 1 and 2 frustrate the expectations of the audience and what is the relationship between these three scenes and the scenes you devised just prior to having worked on them?

(e) *Other stages*. Now shift your 'stage' so that it is at one end of the room and select one of the above scenes to present on the new stage. Remember that the audience can now only view the action from the front and that this should make a difference to the way you present the action. If you need a place from which characters enter the stage space, notice how different this is from when characters entered the arena. Also check with the actors how they feel they should adapt their behaviour to suit the changed conditions. Pay particular attention to the point at which the stage 'ends'. Were you now to frame the acting-area with a kind of picture frame through which the audience watch, you would have a 'proscenium stage', which, quite incorrectly, is often thought of as a 'traditional' form of staging. What does the gap in the frame represent? Without the frame we have an 'open' stage – can you present the three scenes from the previous exercise on either kind of 'end' stage and what is the difference?

Experiment with other types of stage arrangement – for example, a 'thrust' stage projecting out into the audience, or a 'traverse' stage with the audience on either side of a central avenue. Whatever shape you use, discuss ways in which you establish the convention that the stage is the space where the action happens. What happens if actors enter the audience's space or *vice versa*? Have conventions broken down?

(f) *Another space*. Taking these explorations a little further, we can discover what conventions a playwright has decided with regard to his audience. Select a play you have been studying and cast the opening scene. Decide as a group how you would wish to stage it and where you would want that audience to be positioned and then work on a short extract for presentation. When you run through it once provide answers to the following questions:

1   Do the performers pretend that the audience is not there once they have decided how that audience can best see and hear the performance?
2   Do the performers sometimes address the audience directly?
3   Would the performers like the audience to behave as if they were watching a boxing-match, or would they prefer them to sit quietly except when they laugh?
4   Which of the previous three points are determined by the type of play the playwright has created?

(g) *Pause for reflection*. I have suggested a range of activities which are designed to show some of the options and conventions open to the modern playwright. Within the period we have defined as 'modern' you will find playwrights using many kinds of stages. For example, in the late nineteenth and early twentieth century, playwrights were writing for the proscenium stage, creating a picture which the audience viewed through a frame; more often than not it was a picture of domestic life in an interior setting in which actors behaved in many respects as if the audience was not there. The convention was that the audience sat in darkness and watched the goings-on in the room through an imaginary 'fourth wall'. In such a convention it would clearly be unacceptable for one of the actors to speak directly to the audience. The whole proscenium-stage convention has remained popular throughout the modern period and the majority of the plays you study are likely to conform to it in some way.

Some modern directors and playwrights have discovered that the sense of realism that can be achieved by building elaborate, detailed scenery to look like a real room can also be realised by theatre-in-the-round, in which there is real, three-dimensional scenery but only a suggestion of walls or doors. One of the most prolific and successful of contemporary playwrights, Alan Ayckbourn, has all his plays tried out in the round first.

In general, the modern period has seen experiments with every conceivable kind of staging and it will help you considerably in your study of a play if you can discover the playwright's intentions in this respect. The way in which a playwright first imagined his play in the theatre was part of the writing-process and it is likely that his early experience of the play in production contributed to any rewriting he may have done. In workshop activities it is possible to identify the aspects of a play which depend on decisions concerning staging and presentation.

(h) *Further conventions.*

1 Devise a scene in which three couples are talking in their bedrooms about a party they have all attended. All three bedrooms are visible at once, but the conversation may alternate between the three.
2 Devise a further scene in which one of the characters has been rendered semi-conscious so that what the *audience* sees and hears is what that person appears to hear and see.
3 Devise three short scenes at a party that is taking place in three rooms of a house. The second and third scenes begin with characters entering from the room in which the previous scene took place.

These three scenes are rather extreme examples of creating conventions which an audience has to accept in order to make sense of what is happening in a play. They are based on three plays by Alan Ayckbourn, who has shown himself to be a master of creating unusual and effective conventions. His conventions are basically very simple and they work because he has grasped the central fact of theatre that a stage can be transformed into any place, time or thing, provided the perception of the audience can be skilfully manipulated.

Modern playwrights from Ibsen and Strindberg onwards have experimented with many means of exploiting the unique qualities of a live performance; they have thought about types of stage, the behaviour of actors, the relationship between actors and their audience and the universal significance that can be given to the signs and symbols filling the empty space of the stage. As a student you need to identify the way in which a playwright is using the conventions of theatre in his plays.

The link that exists between a play and the place in which it is to be performed may not be immediately apparent to you, so as a conclusion to these initial activities I suggest that you read and discuss the following extract from an article on drama by Shelly Frome, an American university teacher of play-writing. The article is called 'The Basic Ritual':

> To stir up your sense of the theatrical, leave your study for a while and go on a hunt. Take a long walk or a ride in your car. Float downstream in a canoe. Hop on a bicycle. Use any means you like as long as it makes you feel that you're getting far away.
>
> What you're looking for may be indoors or outdoors or both. It's some kind of charged space. It probably reminds you of a stone bull's eye or a dancing ring. But it doesn't have to be circular. It could be a raised platform or a hall inside a weatherbeaten church. It could be back of a ledge overlooking the water. The important thing is that the space transports you and seems timeless. A clearing in the woods will do.
>
> Any area that just is what it is won't do. It won't be quick. It'll be flat, like a warehouse rimmed with cartons of beer or a stage with a box set papered with real wallpaper and cluttered with furniture you've seen on sale. It won't have any resonance.
>
> In your search, think of old rituals that confronted unspoken fears or desires. For instance, try to imagine the winter solstice and the daylight being swallowed up by the night. Could two uncanny people occupy this space, become the day and the night, and play this conflict out, die and be reborn so that a gathering of spectators would know whether or not spring will come again?
>
> Could *any* outsized confrontation or folly be staged here? Let your mind run through some classic struggles – e.g., sons plotting to overthrow their father and take possession of his domain, lovers meeting and discovering they're on opposite sides of a great feud, a queen betrayed by her husband seeking revenge, a fool trying to steal a young bride from an elderly, powerful miser. . . .
>
> Now think of some recent stage-worthy tales. Like a madcap family trying to defy the rules of society. A tired salesman grappling with tired

notions that no longer work. A mismatched pair of men trying to live with each other after failed attempts to live with women. . . .

What you're trying to get in touch with here is a live, dramatic form in suspension that won't quit until something gives way. What you're trying to envision is the kind of arena that will hold it.

(*Speech and Drama*, 1986, pp. 2–3)

This may all seem rather quirky to you and you may even be surprised that someone can actually claim to *teach* playwriting, but Professor Frome has really put his finger on the difference between a play and a work of literature: the play has to happen, and in that sense it is an event with strong ritual qualities. In your workshop activities you have been paring down the ideas of drama until all you have is an empty space and some actors: this is very different from thinking 'A play begins with a text that I have to read', although this is the stage at which you probably joined the process. You need to remember that before that play can have any life you must return in your imagination to the empty space and begin to fill it with the sounds, sights, movements and impressions that the playwright intended. From this point on, then, don't think of the play you are studying as taking place in so and so's house or in such and such a street; think of it rather as taking place on a *stage* which *represents* that place, and think of the characters not as real people but as actors and actresses who are presenting those characters to you.

Some further exercises

The remaining exercises are grouped to make certain points and you are asked both to make sure you have understood both the *point* of the exercise and the instructions before you begin. You will need to have read and studied the play carefully before embarking on these activities.

Character

The object of this section is to deepen your understanding of the characters in the play. The creation of a 'character' has two main phases: the playwright's invention and the actor's invention. During these exercises you will come to see more of the information supplied by the playwright and will discover what happens when an actor takes this material and begins to shape it into a performance.

BEGINNINGS

1   Ideally work in pairs of this exercise. Select two characters from your set play who enter the stage and meet early on in the action so that this is the first time the audience would have seen either of them. Discuss the nature of this meeting – where and when it takes place, how long it is since the characters last met (minutes? hours? years?). Alternatively, select a moment early in the play when two characters make their entrance or are seen on stage for the first time *together*. Again, discuss this situation – how long the characters have known each other, where and when they met, and so on. Now take a character each and *in your own words* tell the other character what you had been doing before you met. Most of the information will be in the text and you may need to check some details before you can do this with confidence – at this stage prompt each other with details that one of you may have forgotten. Discover and discuss how much you need to invent.

2   Try to 'get in role': that is, imagine yourself looking, thinking and sounding like the character you've chosen. Take on that character's past life in your imagination and think of his or her behaviour characteristics. Arrange your working-space to include any essential pieces such as a chair or table but imagine all the rest. Now make your first entrance and as you do so say aloud in your own words what your character is thinking and feeling – notice, this is the 'sub-text' coming to the surface. Think where you have been, what you are anticipating, how you would move. Each member of the group should try this several times, with the others making constructive suggestions.

3   Carrying the previous experience forward, take the text of the play and work on the first entrance/meeting. Use the first few lines of dialogue and all the stage directions that the playwright has provided and try this moment in various ways until you are satisfied that the relationship between the text and the sub-text and between the two characters is

what you really feel the playwright intended. At this stage 'pairs' may wish to come together for a discussion of what has been discovered. Be prepared to learn from each other's experience.

RELATIONSHIPS

1   Select one member of the group to act as chairperson; the rest should each take a character from the play. The chairperson selects a character to sit in the middle of a circle with the others grouped round. Each character in turn now tells the character in the middle the precise nature of his/her relationship with him/her both as the play begins and as it progresses. This will include factual details of birth, family, and so on, but will move on to feelings and attitudes. The chairperson keeps a careful check that all opinions can be supported by the text and may question the characters in the circle. All characters take a turn in the centre.

2   In a group discussion recall incidents in the play when particular tensions arise or appear to surface between two characters. Split the group into pairs and work on short scenes containing these incidents. First read the scene through several times until you are thoroughly familiar with it; then act it out in various ways. Work especially on the physical positioning of the two characters: experiment with and decide on the space between them.

3   In the same scene try speaking the lines with a pause of, say, three seconds between each speech. Use the silence to decide what your character's reaction to the previous speech would be. Gradually increase the length of the pauses but listen even more intently to every word and maintain a very high level of concentration throughout. As you work on this you should find that the lines of thought in the scene become much clearer: you will discover, for example, if your character really *is* listening to the other or whether he or she is actually following a course determined by some other factor. The exercise is difficult at first and will seem very strange until you are used to it.

4   By contrast, play the scene as rapidly as you can, with each speech following on immediately from the next. What effect does this have? Decide by experiment which method creates the tension in the scene and try a combination of both

without warning your partner when you are going to pause
and when you are going to take up a cue quickly.
5   Select another scene in which at least one of the characters
is attempting to ease tension and improve the relationship.
Try some of the experiments already listed and then decide
privately precisely what your character *wants* in this scene –
do not disclose this but now play the scene constantly
bearing that in mind. Discuss the results: did you have to
shift your aims and adopt a different strategy because of the
other character's behaviour? Play the scene again but this
time use your own words. Remember, a character's
behaviour will be governed by his or her wants and needs –
these will be pursued throughout any scene.

EACH CHARACTER'S STORY
1   This is a more lengthy activity which may well extend over
several sessions and could be expanded into a full workshop
production. It begins with group discussion and, ideally,
the group(s) should consist of as many people as there are
characters in the play, but an additional chairperson or
someone who wishes to have a go at directing can always
be accommodated. The activity can also work well if only
the major characters are represented. Start by selecting a
character each and then, in turn, find the point in the play
where each character makes a final appearance. The task is
for all the characters in turn tell their own story *from their
point of view* from their first appearance in the play until their
last. Initially this can be done verbally, but as each
character tells more and more of his or her story it will
rapidly become apparent that the story begins before the
play opens and may, unless the character dies, continue
after it has ended.
2   Each character must then select scenes and speeches which
tell his or her story and, working with the rest of the group,
construct a short play which presents that character's story
from the personal angle. Scenes and speeches may be linked
with improvised dialogue or monologue. For example, after
a short scene from the play illustrating your character's
relationship to another character, you may go on to
describe what you think took place on another occasion.
You may even invent scenes that are not in the play. By

the conclusion of the activity everyone should have participated in every character's story.

3   Use your experience to identify key speeches, and then find ways of linking all the material selected so that the action is continuous. It will, of course, be necessary to make notes and working scripts so that everyone knows what is going on, and each character will need to determine how the space that you have available is to be used to maximum effect. You should concentrate on telling the story in a simple, direct way and decide who and where your audience might be. Sharing this kind of work with other groups can be very useful, but beware of situations in which 'outsiders' offer criticisms of the 'performance': this is not important – it is the exploration and experience that matter. Simple studio lighting, video recording and music can all enhance the work, but they are by no means essential. The 'stories' *can* remain verbal or be written as short stories.

Lines of action

In Chapter 2 we considered the distinction between the overall story-line of a play and the precise action. As you will just have been reminded, the story is of great importance and it is probably what grips people most in a theatrical performance, but what is *actually going on* in a play, the issues being explored and the questions being raised, has to do with the play's action. Discovering the various levels on which the action takes place can be quite difficult, because beneath the surface events are many complex factors and lines of action. The play is the sum total of all the various lines of action, so discovering what those lines of action are will help towards a complete understanding.

The following activities are designed to help you discover the lines of action pursued by different characters in the play you are studying. One method will be to outline a situation around which you can improvise scenes which demonstrate some of the tensions and real aims beneath the surface. This technique has been used with great effectiveness by the contemporary theatre director Charles Marowitz. He engages in intensive periods of study with his actors in an attempt to achieve the most intelligent and truthful production possible. Marowitz has worked on a number of the modern plays mentioned in this book, and I propose using two examples of his work (described in his book *The Act of Being* (1978)) to suggest similar workshop activities for you. Even if you are not studying these particular plays, I would urge you to work through the examples and then move on to devise similar activities for your set plays.

Look Back in Anger, by John Osborne is a play about a working-class young man who has been to university and marries a girl from the upper middle class. Jimmy, the young man, takes every opportunity to attack the scale of values for which he thinks his wife's family and upbringing stand.

After several detailed readings decide what seem to be the major issues raised by the play and devise the improvisations which explore lines of action related to them. Marowitz identifies 'Class attitudes in England – particularly those obtaining in the mid 1950s' as the main issue raised by *Look Back in Anger* and suggests the following three improvisations concerned with social class.

1   Situation and surface action: working-class young person who has had a good education but has little social status meets an old school friend who has been incredibly successful and now moves in much higher social circles. The successful friend invites working-class man/woman to some function or place to talk about old times.

  Friend's action is to flaunt his/her new success to impress working-class person, who had tended to behave in a 'superior' way at school because of academic achievements.

  Working-class person's action is to accept the invitation because of a mixture of interest and resentment: he/she tries then to deflate wealthy friend's ego and belittle what is being held up as social achievement.

2   Situation and surface action: working-class young man/woman with good education accepts invitation to supper party from wealthy, upper-middle-class parents of girl/boy friend.

  Family's action is to make working-class guest feel as uncomfortable as possible in an attempt to make their son/daughter see that their friendship is impossible.

Working-class person's action is to mock the values and life-style of the parents.

Son's/daughter's action is to try to bring together the two conflicting forces.

3   Situation and surface action: working-class person brought before magistrates for drunken conduct which has led to release of class prejudice.

Magistrates' action is to probe the offender's attitude to the establishment.

Working-class person's action is to demonstrate contempt for authority as represented by the magistrates.

Death of a Salesman, by Arthur Miller, has already been used as an example several times in this book and you will remember that it concerns a father who is disillusioned with his job and disappointed with his two sons. Charles Marowitz began his work on the play by the kind of detailed study I have outlined in this book and decided that some of the major issues of the play were 'Illusions of success fostered by misconceived social goals and disparities of consciousness between . . . one generation and another'. The improvisations devised were designed to explore:

1   the American ideal of free enterprise and the pressure to sell yourself to the company;
2   the tensions between a father and a son who have totally different concepts of success and yet remain devoted to each other;
3   the class of values between the 'establishment' and what the opposition sees as bogus.

You can see that what this type of improvisation is trying to achieve is to get to the root of the problems that affect a play's action without getting bogged down in the precise events and text of the play itself. This enables students and actors to approach the play refreshed and with new insights which they can apply to the detailed business of rehearsing or analysing a scene.

Having considered the above examples, your task now is to find similar work for the play you are studying. Begin in group discussion by identifying certain key issues with which the play deals. Almost certainly they will derive from the threat to social order you have noticed earlier. Now decide on some simple situations with which you are reasonably familiar or can easily imagine containing characters who share some of the attributes and attitudes of those in the play. Act out the situations and decide on a line of action for each character.

Find scenes in the set play in which similar lines of action take place beneath the surface events. Rehearse them as 'polished' readings with all the activity suggested by the playwright.

Take a short scene from the play and in groups of two or three work through the text reading the lines and obeying every single stage direction and indication of movement in the dialogue. Take great care to set up your dance with all the furniture and other properties either used or suggested. When you have been through the scene, discuss the reasons *why* your character was given certain moves and 'business' to do; persist until you find a satisfactory answer which springs from the 'action' of your character. Pay particular attention also to what your character does and thinks when *not* speaking.

Shapes and rhythms

Like a piece of music, a play has a form which is made up of various sections each with their own tempi, rhythms and climaxes. These patterns are not really evident from the written page but are an essential figure of the playwright's craft. Workshop exercises such as the following will reveal many of the aspects of form in the play.

1   It will be obvious at a glance which characters speak *most* in a play but it is more important to discover who takes the initiative. Take a number of short scenes between two characters: remembering all the work you have done so far, read the scenes through carefully (aloud) and decide which character really dictates the way the scene goes. Who controls the speed? Who usually speaks first? Try to discover how the scene builds to a climax and what constitutes a key *moment* in the scene.

2   Try once more to discover the *pace* of the scene: what is the

effect of the moment(s) you have identified? Once you are familiar with the text, act out the scenes with all the activity that the text and stage directions demand. How would you ensure that the important climax is appreciated by an audience? How is that moment achieved? By facial expression, change of volume, movement? Or is there some elaborate 'business' specified which the audience must see clearly?

3   Work through an entire act or sequence by dividing it into scenes for which different members of the group are responsible. Each scene must have its own clearly defined climax or significant moment when the action changes pace. Act out each scene in turn and at the conclusion of each scene discuss (a) how the action has advanced; (b) what is now known that was not known before; (c) how the interest is sustained from one scene to the next. Draw a graph-like diagram showing the way in which the tension rises and falls throughout the scene, representing each climax as a high point on the graph. Repeat this process for the entire play.

4   Improvise a short scene, of no more than five minutes' duration, which contains the essence of the whole play – all the main events must either be shown or suggested so that you end up with a very clear idea of what the major climaxes are. This apparently ridiculous exercise can be very valuable. I once worked with a group of students whose understanding of Shakespeare's *King Lear* suddenly broke new ground after they had constructed a five-minute version of the play!

A more subtle kind of division than those we have already explored is the unit or 'beat' (as Charles Marowitz calls it). Think back to the idea that each character or set of characters has a distinctive line of action arising from that character's/ group's wants. As a character plays his or her line of action, other characters will respond and adapt their own line of action accordingly. For example, character A may be trying to make character B reveal a secret. Character B, who may originally have intended asking A for something, now begins to try to find a way to bring the meeting to an end; and so on. Each small group of actions which relate closely to each other constitutes a unit within a scene: that unit may last a few minutes or may continue for much of the scene. You can only detect the shift from one unit to the next in practical work. That is why I have urged you to establish 'moments': a moment is an *event* in time and space; not a word on a page but something which happens on a stage. The small units or beats may be defined by the duration of a particular mood or attitude. When it changes, the performance has moved into another phase. Bearing all this in mind, try the following further exercise.

5   Work together on a selected extract from a modern play, such as the piece from *A Taste of Honey* on p. 36. Divide the extract into 'beats' taking particular notice of how the character you are reading adapts his/her line of action in response to other characters.

Activities

In Chapter 2 we noted the distinction between the *action* of the play, which embraces all that occurs during a play's performance, and specific *activities*: the things which actors and actresses *do*. These activities are not suggested by the playwright to fill time or even simply to make the characters seem 'natural'. Modern playwrights tend to give more precise instructions in this direction than their predecessors. If you have studied Pinter's *The Dumb Waiter* or Beckett's *Waiting for Godot*, for example, you will remember very precise activities involving the taking off and putting on of shoes. By indulging in various kinds of activity a character reveals things about his/her personality and aims, and makes clearer what the action of the play is at that point. An activity may be so all-embracing that the whole body is involved (as in fighting or in creeping round a room) or may be used to accompany some important action (as in fiddling with a pen whilst nervously waiting for someone, or pouring a drink in order to make someone feel at ease). Activities must 'happen' in order to be appreciated as part of a playwright's art and the following exercises will highlight this aspect of drama.

1   Act out all the activities in this extract from Pinter's *The Caretaker*. Aston has left Davies, an old tramp, in his room. The room is filled with junk and Davies begins to explore it. What is the effect of all this activity? How does it enrich and clarify the action at this point in the play?

DAVIES *stands still. He waits a few seconds, then goes to the door, opens it, looks out, closes it, stands with his back to it, turns swiftly, opens it, looks out, comes back, closes the door, finds the keys in his pocket, tries one, tries the other, locks the door. He looks about the room. He then goes quickly to* ASTON's *bed, bends, brings out the pair of shoes and examines them.*

Not a bad pair of shoes. Bit pointed.

He puts them back under the bed. He examines the area by ASTON's *bed, picks up a vase and looks into it, then picks up a box and shakes it.*

Screws!

He sees paint buckets at the top of the bed, goes to them, and examines them.

Paint. What's he going to paint?

He puts the bucket down, comes to the centre of the room, looks up at bucket, and grimaces.

I'll have to find out about that. [*He crosses right, and picks up a blow-lamp.*] He's got some stuff in here. [*He picks up the Buddha and looks at it.*] Full of stuff. Look at all this. [*His eye falls on the piles of papers.*] What's he got all those papers for? Damn pile of papers.

He goes to a pile and touches it. The pile wobbles. He steadies it.

Hold it, hold it!

He holds the pile and pushes the papers back into place.

The door opens.

MICK *comes in, puts the key in his pocket, and closes the door silently. He stands at the door and watches* DAVIES.

What's he got all these papers for? [DAVIES *climbs over the rolled carpet to the blue case.*] Had a sheet and pillow ready in here. [*He opens the case.*] Nothing. [*He shuts the case.*] Still, I had a sleep though. I don't make no noises. [*He looks at the window.*] What's this?

He picks up another case and tries to open it. MICK *moves upstage, silently.*

Locked. [*He puts it down and moves downstage.*] Must be something in it. [*He picks up a sideboard drawer, rummages in the contents, then puts it down.*]

MICK *slides across the room.*

DAVIES *half turns,* MICK *seizes his arm and forces it up his back.* DAVIES *screams.*

Uuuuuuuhhh! Uuuuuuuhhh! What! What! What! Uuuuuuuhhh!

MICK *swiftly forces him to the floor, with* DAVIES *struggling, grimacing, whimpering and staring.*

MICK *holds his arm, puts his other hand to his lips, then puts his hand to* DAVIES's *lips.* DAVIES *quietens.* MICK *lets him go.* DAVIES *writhes.* MICK *holds out a warning finger. He then squats down to regard* DAVIES. *He regards him, then stands looking down on him.* DAVIES *massages his arm, watching* MICK. MICK *turns slowly to look at the room. He goes to* DAVIES's *bed and uncovers it. He turns, goes to the clothes horse and picks up* DAVIES's *trousers.* DAVIES *starts to rise.* MICK *presses him down with his foot and stands over him. Finally he removes his foot. He examines the trousers and throws them back.* DAVIES *remains on the floor, crouched.* MICK *slowly goes to the chair, sits, and watches* DAVIES, *expressionless. Silence.*

MICK. What's the game?

Curtain,

(Methuen, 1967, pp. 27–9)

2   Take an act from your set play and underline all the suggested activity in the script. In your group take turns at being a director who has to explain to the actor/actress playing the part the significance of the activities. Rehearse the act in manageable units as if the cast of the play were trying out the action for the first time.

3   Select a convenient place from which you can observe other people. Pick a couple of people to watch carefully and for a given time – say ten minutes – making a note of all their activities. Compare notes with your fellow students, then discuss the significance of the activities in relation to the action you have observed. For example, you may watch someone who carries out a whole series of meticulously careful activities or you may see two people meeting or trying to attract attention – you will hardly ever see anyone remain perfectly still. What is the purpose of the activities you observe?

4   Take the following piece of dialogue and turn it into a one-minute scene with clearly defined action and detailed activity:

CHARACTER A [*knocks on door*]. Excuse me!
CHARACTER B. Come in!

The given circumstances

This rather strange expression comes from the famous Russian director Stanislavski, who was particularly associated with the plays of Chekhov, a contemporary of Ibsen. Stanislavski's work with actors remains the most influential approach to the interpretation of texts in the theatre, and it is well worth studying the way in which he set about bringing a play to life in his productions. His great concern for truthful portrayal of characters led him to consider the way in which people change according to circumstances. There is a great danger in talking about 'character' in a play as if this were something that remained static: when in studying Shakespeare we talk about the 'character of Macbeth', for example, we might fall into the trap of imagining a neat package we can write about in an essay, but in real life we know that Macbeth the husband and Macbeth the father are very different from Macbeth the king.

The circumstances in which a character may find him or herself are almost limitless. A character is surrounded by an *environment*, *events* and *other characters*, and it is the interaction with all of these which creates the tension and interest in drama.

1 Take a scene from your play which involves characters in entering a room. Arrange the stage space to represent the room, then take a character each and survey the room, speaking your thoughts aloud. Is the room familiar to you? Is it welcoming or hostile? Where have you just been? What is outside the room? Question each character about his/her reaction to the room and how he/she feels as on entering and leaving it.

2 Select a contrasting environment – maybe an outdoor location or another room and improvise your character's reaction to it. Find scenes in your play which use different locations *or* discuss why the playwright has restricted the action to a single space. What features of the environment change during the course of the play?

3 Now turn your attention from the physical world enveloping a character to the social world. Select a scene with two characters and act out the scene. When you have done so ask the following questions. What do I now know about the other character that I did not know before? What is the consequence of the fact that I know *nothing* more or of what I *do* now know? Has either of us been trying to hide anything? If so, what tactics were employed?

4 Select incidents from the play which demonstrate how your character behaves differently according to changed circumstances. In small groups present a selection of scenes as rehearsed readings to illustrate the behavioural patterns of the main characters.

Readers' theatre

Unless you have had a great deal of time to spare, it is unlikely that you will have had the opportunity to learn a role for performance, in whole or part, and your work will either have been improvised or have taken the form of a reading. In an attempt to come nearer to the idea of a performance, many teachers and students in the United States have realised the value of what they call 'readers' theatre'. This is a carefully devised and rehearsed mode of presentation in which the words are read by a group of performers with close attention to characterisation, qualities of speech and oral interpretation. There is no physical action as such, although a great deal of thought goes into arranging the readers in an effective way: they may each sit on stools in a spotlight against a neutral background, for instance, and they may decide to dress in a simple, unifying manner, all in black perhaps.

An American professor of readers' theatre once explained that the drama actually occurs in the imaginations of the audience as if there is a meeting-point between the sound of the performers' words and the inner eye of the listener. In order to create this imagined performance, the readers will read not only the dialogue but also some, if not all, of the stage directions, and will also ensure that all the music and sound-effects are cued in at the appropriate time. The result can be quite remarkably stimulating and has a great deal in common with one of the most formative influences on contemporary playwrights, radio drama.

1   In groups large enough to cover all the cast requirements, devise a readers'-theatre presentation of your set play(s). Groups could take an act each and present the play in several parts. The roles should be prepared with all possible attention to the text, sub-text, scene shape and other issues which we have worked on, and a very high level of concentration should be maintained throughout rehearsals and performance. This is *not* like 'reading round the class': the onus on each participant is to play the line of his or her action and enable a listener to visualise the character's activity clearly.

2   Present your interpretation as a radio drama by initially

recording the readers'-theatre performance. How will you deal with the absence of stage directions in the spoken text? Discuss the effect of removing the visual element from drama: how does the absence of visual signs and symbols restrict the performance?

We have by no means exhausted all the possibilities of studying a play through active involvement, but many of the other activities I could suggest would presuppose that you were working towards a full production of the play. This is an ideal situation which, unfortunately, is rarely possible, but you should *imagine* at every stage in your work on a play that ultimately you will be needing to make those decisions which will result in a performance in the theatre.

7

Characters and themes

In this short chapter I want to draw together two of the main strands, that is, characters and themes – that have been running through all my suggestions for study. This is because it is the characters and themes which make a play interesting and because both these aspects of drama are favourite topics for essays and exam questions. I am going to begin with some general comments about characters and then go on to suggest ways of refining your understanding of them. I shall then examine the way in which the characters and themes of a play interrelate, and offer some guidance about identifying aspects of a theme.

By the time you have studied a play carefully, following all the steps I have outlined, you should feel as if you know all the characters personally. You should be able to talk about them as you could about a close friend or relation. The one thing which you will realise about people you know well is that they are very complex, and the same will be true of characters in a play. The playwright offers a view of the world and of the process of being alive; that view will reflect the fact that life is a strangely complicated affair. The more you know someone, the more you discover about a character, the more you find that that person is full of contradictions, inconsistencies, prejudices, mixed motives, beliefs and other attractive and less attractive features. No simple statement will ever adequately sum up a complete character, although you may well be able to sum up important *aspects* of a character.

The characters with whom a dramatist has chosen to people his or her play take on a life of their own once you begin to watch their reaction to other characters and to the situation in which they find themselves. Unlike the characters in a novel, however, characters in a play are meant to be realised on stage, and actors and actresses may portray the same characters in very different ways. One actress, for example, might show Shaw's St Joan as a tough, no-nonsense girl who simply brushes obstacles aside, whereas another might portray her as more introspective and tentative. Your job is to take the evidence given in the text of the play and, bearing in mind what happens when the text comes to life, form your own judgement.

The first solid thing you can do is to accumulate information about a character. I always do this by making a table of two columns for each character. In the first column I note down all that I know about a character and in the second column how I obtained that information. Both Arthur Miller and George Bernard Shaw tend to provide brief biographical details about characters as they are introduced, so, after noting those details in the first column, I would write 'playwright's note Act I, scene i' (or whatever) in my second column. Other information is revealed by characters in speeches about themselves, in speeches by others and during the course of conversation. There will be startling revelations that may change the whole direction of the play, but there will also be a lot of apparently trivial detail which will gradually build up a picture. I always make a further sub-division of my table: alongside all the straightforward facts such as 'He is 45' or 'She has been married for 5 years' I write a figure '1'. Beside all facts about the past, such as 'Used to be in love with Mary', I write a figure '2'; and details of attitudes, such as 'Regards women's place as in the kitchen', I label '3'. This is a useful division because it enables me to see at a glance the different sets of facts which I would want to group together if I had to write about a character.

In my second column, where I put these numbers, I have begun to show *how* a playwright provides us with information, which is really another way of saying how he or she 'creates character'. I haven't yet got the full profile of a character, but I have already accumulated valuable evidence which I can use in an essay to support any statement I might want to make. If, for instance, I want to make a claim that a character has a certain set of attitudes, I can now cite examples to back up my contention.

Much more interesting things happen to characters when they have to make choices. Even the apparently most trivial choices lead to further questions. If I decide to have vegetarian nut roast for my lunch instead of roast beef, it may be because I believe it is wrong to kill animals, or that high intakes of animal fat are damaging to my health. On the other hand it may be that the vegetarian meal is the cheaper of the two or that I prefer the taste of nuts to that of beef. There are still several other factors which may govern my choice, and you can't assume anything until you know a great deal more about my attitudes, my economic position and my tastes.

Now, you could say that my preference for nut roast relates to the whole 'theme' or 'issue' of vegetarianism and this is one way in which playwrights can highlight a particular question, but that is not an argument I want to pursue at this point. What does emerge from this simple example is a variety of ways of looking at my 'character'. If my refusal to eat meat stems from the fact that I am squeamish about it, this tells you something about my psychological make-up. You may also discover that I am particularly fond of animals and that I cannot bear the thought of any kind of suffering; in fact you can carry on trying to account for my actions (in this case a choice) in all kinds of psychological ways and you will be looking for other evidence from all my actions to fill out your view. You can see that this is what you do when you study a character in the play: you see that character involved in a series of choices and actions, and from these you make deductions about the character's psychological tendencies. If you note down examples of the different kinds of action that a character performs, you are well on your way to building up a case study of that person with suitable examples.

But, returning to my example, if you decide that my objection has purely *moral* grounds, then you will have learned something about my attitudes and you may wish to discover if these are part of a wider set of moral or religious convictions to which I adhere. In Shaw's play *Major Barbara* the heroine subscribes to the set of beliefs espoused by members of the Salvation Army. These include a rigid teetotalism and an involvement with caring for the underprivileged. All Barbara's decisions are made in the light of these convictions. For every character you study you should recognise the scheme of ideas to which he or she subscribes. It may be possible to summarise this code briefly; you might, for instance, say that Willy Loman subscribes to the 'American Dream', or that Hilda in Ibsen's *The Master Builder* is a 'bluestocking', but remember that this does not tell you everything about them.

Finally, to exhaust my example, imagine that my decision to eat vegetarian food is simply an economic decision: it's cheaper than meat. On further investigation this may tell you that I'm always very careful with my money but it may also reveal that I'm poor. In other words, my actions are dictated by necessity. When you consider a character you should list those external pressures which make that character act in a particular way. Many of Brecht's plays show characters who act out of the need to survive; they cannot afford the luxury of moral scruples because the choice is between survival and extermination. You may argue a person should never compromise his or her convictions and should even be prepared to die for them. Becket chooses this path in *Murder in the Cathedral* and becomes a martyr and tragic hero; Brecht however, puts the choice to the audience and points up all the pressures which capitalist society places upon its members.

You will see that, as you build up a set of ideas as to *why* a character acts as he or she does, there are many factors to be taken into consideration. In the study of modern drama we have to remember that playwrights and we ourselves are likely to use rational scientific explanations for human behaviour. During the period I have defined as 'modern', the sciences of psychology and sociology have increasingly taken over from religion as a means of accounting for people's individual and group conduct. We now tend to think, for example, that our subconscious mind in some way stores experiences from the past and shapes our present behaviour. Thus many modern plays are greatly concerned with the past and its sometimes ghostly presence in the present. Plays also show an interest in the nature of dreams and in various kinds of neurosis. Explaining behaviour in these terms was entirely unknown to Shakespeare, for example, and many dramatists from early periods would have been more likely to attribute actions to divine providence or astrological causes. Similarly, we now tend to describe society in political and economic terms and are very concerned about the effects of class, technology and various forms of government. The erosion of religious belief, the impact of two world wars and the more recently acquired potential for the human race to destroy itself have all deeply affected the way in which modern dramatists have portrayed people trying to live in the world. What I am anxious to underline here is that modern drama takes account of all the varying factors which are seen to shape human life, so that when you study a character from a play you are likely to find them provided with motives, attitudes, behavioural characteristics and situations which can be investigated and, largely, explained in these terms.

One particularly important factor to note is the relationship of each character to another. I usually help myself by representing this as a diagram. For each character I draw a small circle with his or her name in it. I then join the circles by drawing arrows with an appropriate key word such as 'distrusts' beside it – so, if A distrusts B but B loves A, part of my diagram looks like this:

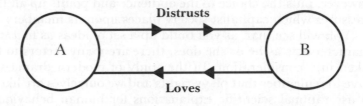

There are many uses to which you can put such a 'sociogram', and it's worth your taking a few minutes to experiment with the relationships which you can show. You eventually build up a complicated diagram that resembles something from atomic physics and this only reinforces the very complex nature of human life. The extension of this is to recognise that characters adopt different strategies according to whom they are with. When B is with A, for instance, B's behaviour will be governed partially by the fact that he or she loves A.

I hope I have said enough to convince you that when you speak of a 'character' you are describing a great deal more than a person who happens to speak certain lines. You should go through the play now with this chapter fresh in your mind and make a set of notes on each of the main characters. You should already have drawn up a table of information and to this you should add any other points that I have caused you to think about. If you are working on the play in a practical way, these notes could form the basis of the ideas a director would give the actors and actresses playing the characters, but they will also serve as revision notes and provide valuable points for your essays. Every point you make should have an example beside it.

What should also have emerged in this chapter is that the problems and predicaments with which the characters become entangled are invariably linked to questions larger than the characters themselves. When Mother Courage in Brecht's play refuses to recognise her own son at the moment of his death, it isn't simply her dilemma which we recognise: it is the whole theme of suffering, survival and expediency. In the same way, when we watch the behaviour of the characters in Shaw's plays *Heartbreak House* and *Misalliance*, we are seeing a microcosm of Edwardian England, England floundering around in a kind of dream before the First World War and, as in the symbol of the conservatory in *Misalliance*, living in a very fragile peace. Shaw's and Stoppard's characters talk a great deal and will often draw attention to the themes they are exploring – problems of class or of the nature of language itself, perhaps. One of the attractions of drama is that it is capable of dealing with very complicated issues, and one of the pleasures of studying a play is to be able to recognise the underlying themes.

That is why I have left this to the end. You have been through all the detail and now, as my tutor used to say to me, you can 'relax and expand'. Students so often fail at this final stage because they are afraid to say, 'Well, I've got all this detail, but what really are the issues and themes raised by this play?' Some recent examination questions illustrate this: examples I have in front of me suggest that *Waiting for Godot* is 'about the realities of everyday life – half understanding and non-communicating'; that 'Ethics is a complicated business' is relevant to Stoppard's *Professional Foul*; or that 'To do the right deed for the wrong reason' is a 'key to the central theme of *Murder in the Cathedral*'. Notice how the questions you are asked to discuss either take a key phrase from the text and ask you to reflect on how that gives clues to what the play is really about, or simply make a statement which you are asked to consider. In either case you need to have reduced your final view of the play to a few strong statements which seem to you to sum up the essence. Once you have done that privately, after a lot of reflection, compare your statements with those of critics and the sort of quotations you will find on exam papers. Remember, your opinion is as valid as anyone else's provided you can back it up with solid evidence. This brings us to the whole question of writing essays and tackling examinations, and this will be the substance of the concluding chapter.

8

Exams and essays

WRITING an essay in an examination or as part of course work ought to be an enjoyable conclusion to a period of study. Examiners are anxious to share your enthusiasm for drama and, as many examiners' reports reveal, are quick to notice if you have gained little enjoyment from your work. The questions they set test your ability to enter into and think seriously about the world of the play and there is never any attempt to confuse or mystify you. Examiners are very human, and their relief and pleasure when they find an answer which genuinely answers the question and shows that the candidate has engaged the issues of the play is considerable.

This short chapter is designed to help you in writing essays and exam answers. I am going to assume that the process is the same for both, although, obviously, outside the exam situation you have more planning-time and can write at greater length. You should remember that examiners are perfectly aware of this fact, and they are certainly not going to set you an exam question that requires more than about four or five sides to answer. You can also be sure that no question is going to require you to write about every aspect of a play. The logical steps you should go through in responding to any essay title are the same, and so the advice I give should cover all your written responses.

Exams in modern drama invariably consist of two main kinds of question. The first kind asks you a direct question about *the issues of the play, the characters or an aspect of the dramatist's technique*. There may also be questions of this kind which relate to more than one of these topics. For example,

How successfully does Miller present Willy Loman's increasingly weak grip on his life in *Death of a Salesman*?

is a question about Miller's technique *and* a character. This does not necessarily make it more difficult. Questions of this kind will also often contain a quotation, either from the play itself or from a critic, and you will be asked to discuss the quotation in relation to your understanding of the play. A question of this type which is really asking about the issues in the play is

> 'Beckett's plays are sad because he is obsessed by human despair, by reflecting on man's inability even to make a decision, much less carry it out.' Discuss this remark in relation to *Waiting for Godot*.

Don't be put off by the *length* of such questions: they are no more difficult than the short ones, such as

> Are the characters of *Waiting for Godot* sufficiently differentiated?

which comes from the same examination paper!

All the questions I have discussed so far, particularly those containing a quotation, have the advantage of identifying for you the issues you are to think about. No one is going to ask you a question about every aspect of the play, and the *question itself* will define for you the area to which you must limit yourself. This is a very good reason for reading the question extremely carefully instead of floundering around hoping to hit upon the right topic by chance. I need to say some very important things about reading questions, but before I do I must mention the other main type of question: *an extract from a play on which you are asked to comment in some way*. This kind of question is increasingly popular as a means of allowing students to show what they can derive from reading a piece of dramatic text. Obviously it involves more reading-time and may thus lead to shorter answers, but it demands a rather different approach from the first kind of question and I shall deal with it at the end of this chapter.

There are three points I want you to remember *whatever* kind of question you are tackling. First, *there are no preconceived correct answers*. Examiners do not have a series of 'right' and 'wrong' categories, except for facts which you might use to support your argument. Examination questions provide you with an opportunity to show your understanding and appreciation of what you have been studying and, provided you can back up what you say with evidence from the play, your opinion is as valid as anyone else's. Examiners are interested in and want to know your personal response to a play, and your job is to show that you've allowed yourself to become involved in exploring the world which the playwright has created.

Second, you must remember that you are writing about a *play*. At this stage this seems so obvious that it hardly needs stating, but time and again examiners remark in their reports that candidates forget the stagecraft of the writer and the impact of the play on an audience.

Third, it's not a good idea to suggest by the tone of your answer that you consider the examiner to be an idiot – in other words, your basic answer should not be 'This is a stupid question!' Questions are set and checked after lengthy deliberations and any statements contained in them may well provoke you into strong disagreement. They will put forward a reasoned viewpoint and you must counteract with cool argument any view with which you differ.

Let's imagine that you have decided to tackle the following question about T. S. Eliot's *Murder in the Cathedral*. It doesn't matter for the sake of our discussion if you don't know the play, for I shall say sufficient to guide you through it.

> 'Who killed the Archbishop?' Comment on the effect and significance of the knights' speeches to the audience after the murder.

This question begins with a quotation from the play itself and it immediately points to the issue with which you are dealing. As it stands, the quotation suggests that there is some kind of mystery about the death of the Archbishop, but when you know the play you are aware that the murder of the Archbishop is carried out by the four knights in full view of the audience, and yet it is one of those knights who asks, 'Who killed the Archbishop?' When the knight asks that question he is obviously not asking precisely which knight struck the fatal blow; the question is asked for rhetorical effect and as a prelude to a number of speeches in which the knights address the audience, justifying their actions and insisting not only that the Archbishop's death was necessary but also that the audience too were to blame. So in a remarkable way the keyword in that quotation is *Who*, and I would underline it.

If you look carefully at the second half of the question, you can see that by underlining the two key issues on which you are asked to comment there are really two questions:

> Comment on the *effect* and *significance* of the knights' speeches to the audience after the murder.

Thus we could reword what you are first asked to do like this:

> Bearing in mind the question of guilt for the Archbishop's death, comment on the *effect* of the knights' speeches to the audience after the murder.

You may also decide that, remembering that this is a *play*, the words *to the audience* are particularly important because they point to something quite specific about how the dramatist wanted his play performed. The second question which I have identified by underlining a key word concerns the *significance* of the knight's speeches, which is not the same as the *effect*. You cannot hope to answer both questions at the same time.

The rule then, is

1 *Read the question very carefully and underline key words*
2 *Create separate questions from the key words*

Try this out on another question about the same play, bearing in mind that at a recent conference of chief examiners the word 'Discuss' was taken to include 'Investigate or examine by argument; sift and debate; give reasons for and against; examine the implications!'

> Discuss the role and presentation of the Chorus in *Murder in the Cathedral*.

Well, you should have underlined the words *role* and *presentation* to indicate the component questions, and possibly *Chorus* to remind yourself whom you are dealing with. You may ask, 'What's the point of all this? I can see I have to read the question carefully, but why all this underlining?' The answer is that you don't just *read* the question: you *analyse* it. In order to see why, read this first paragraph from a student's answer to the question about 'Who killed the Archbishop?'

'Who killed the Archbishop?' is a quotation from one of the speeches of the four knights in *Murder in the Cathedral*. All four knights have very different characters and they each make a speech in which they explain why the Archbiship had to be killed. They end up by trying to make the audience feel guilty and then tell them to disperse quietly. Eliot said he wrote the play as an anti-nazi play and the four knights became like authorities in a police state who try to justify violence and say that it's necessary. One of the knights suspects that Thomas Becket was responsible for his own death.

I'm sure you can sense that this has not begun very well. The student has some interesting things to say and he or she has obviously read the play and something about it, but the answer already lacks any form of structure. Already the details of the question, the *effect* and the *significance*, have become confused and almost forgotten. Each sentence strikes out hopefully in a new direction without much reference to the previous sentence. The student seems to be looking for a way forward and every now and again slips in a carefully learned fact in the hope of impressing the examiner. You will probably agree with me that the answer doesn't seem to be going anywhere and that there is no sense in which the student is mounting a well-considered argument. At the same time you may also feel that there is some merit in the fact that the quotation has been successfully identified and that the student obviously knows the incident to which the question refers.

Had the student analysed the question, however, the response would have been so much better. The analysis will help you to shape your essay and that shape should be outlined in the **first paragraph**. A brief, clear statement of how you intend to tackle the answer is the best way to begin your answer. You will remember that I underlined three key words. The first was in the quotation itself, which is *not* the real question but identifies an issue: '*Who* killed the Archbishop?' The other two words underlined are *effect* and *significance*, each of which identifies a different question. The plan for my essay ought to be that I first acknowledge the quotation as a major issue in the play, then go on to show how the knights' speeches have an *effect*, and then discuss what *significance* they have as the question 'Who killed the Archbishop?' is posed. My opening paragraph might read thus:

> After the audience has watched the ritual killing of Becket in *Murder in the Cathedral* the knights suddenly turn to them and, addressing them directly, pose the question 'Who killed the Archbishop?' In this answer I intend to discuss the effect of this moment in the theatre when, for the second time, the audience is involved in the action of the play. I shall then go on to examine the significance of the knights' suggestion that the murder of Becket was necessary and inevitable and that the audience must share the guilt.

You can see that I have already decided on the two main parts of my essay and have thought clearly about the word *effect*, so that I realise that it has to do with the performance of the play. I indicate that Eliot has already used this technique once, and this will enable me to make comparisons in the following paragraphs. I have also said something about the nature of Becket's death: I have described it as a 'ritual killing' and this will help me to explain the effect of the very different kind of action which follows it. I have given enough pointers for me to pick up in subsequent paragraphs. I have also revealed that I have spotted the difference between the *effect* which happens in a moment and the *significance*, which concerns the themes and issues of the play. Notice that, brief as this paragraph is, it says enough to set up rest of the essay and help me organise my thoughts.

My **second paragraph** might begin something like this:

> The effect of the knights' speeches on the audience is one of shock, for the speeches are totally unexpected. During the murder of Becket the knights have enacted a ritual brought out by their own doggerel verse and the great lament of the Chorus. Now, however, the nature of the action suddenly changes and becomes realistic. The language also changes from verse to colloquial prose, so the experience of the audience moves from witnessing a remote historical event to being directly confronted by the implications of the action. Eliot has in some ways prepared the audience for this moment by his use of direct address in Becket's sermon, which itself also bears on the question of 'Who Killed the Archbishop?'

You will see that this is a simple paragraph which has three elements. First there is my *statement* 'The effect of the Knights' speeches on the audience is one of shock', to which I have added a reinforcing statement, that 'the speeches are totally unexpected'. It's important to begin with a clear, unambiguous statement that says exactly what you want it to say, and here there is no doubting that I've made a bold assertion. Now I must *justify* what I have said, so the next element in my paragraph is a section of *evidence* which explains why the knights' speeches have the effect they do. I have chosen to concentrate at this point on change – change from ritual to realism, change from verse to prose, and change from detached spectator to involved participant; in other words, I have drawn upon *examples from the play* to show why this constitutes a theatrical shock. My use of these examples constitutes a brief *discussion* of the topic. The examples are meaningless unless I do offer some discussion, and in this instance what I have done is to take the idea of shock brought about by sudden change and then pointed to different kinds of change to which the audience is subjected. My penultimate sentence also offers a *conclusion* to this very short section of the argument. I have moved from saying that the initial effect is a shock and that this has a further effect – that of making the audience feel involved in a contemporary issue. Finally, taking the central idea of the paragraph, I have moved towards another point in the argument in a *linking* statement which naturally leads me on to a further paragraph.

In that **third paragraph** I should examine Beckett's sermon in the play and its effect (it consists of a speech directed straight at the audience as if they were members of the cast), and then briefly explain *how* that speech contrasts with the knights' speeches and how the contrast adds to the sense of shock and so emphasises the question of the Archbishop's death. I should then be ready to move into a **fourth paragraph**, which would begin to examine more fully the individual speeches of the knights, always remembering it is their *effect* which is my chief concern.

Successful paragraphing is really the key to essay writing and your paragraphs should lead naturally from one to another. As the essay progresses you must take straight-forward, honest statements about your response to the play and develop the argument you want to make as a reasoned answer to the question you have chosen. A paragraph is simply a unit of thought in which you make statements and justify them in a logical sequence. Many of your paragraphs will be of the simple kind I have just described, but you may need to deal with rather more complex issues which demand an extension of this simple form. This would be quite likely when it came to dealing with the **second part** of our sample question, the part which asks about the *significance* of the knights' speeches. Let's suppose that I have decided that the final speech of the First Knight, which includes a suggestion to 'disperse quietly' and a thinly veiled threat, is confirmation that Eliot is portraying a police state. I also want to link this to the fact that loyalty to the state has been an issue throughout the play. This is an altogether more complicated affair than the simple paragraph can accommodate; so the paragraph discussing the subject may need to be quite long and will need to contain several sets of evidence and comment before moving to a conclusion. So the shape of my paragraph will be as follows.

(a) A statement about the idea of a police state.
(b) Various pieces of evidence from the play – perhaps confined to the knights' speeches.
(c) Discussion of this evidence.
(d) More evidence, which uses other parts of the play.
(e) Discussion of this set of evidence.
(f) Conclusion which draws together both discussions.
(g) Link to the next paragraph.

You will notice that in my example I have assumed that I can quote the final speech of the First Knight accurately, and this is because in my earlier study of the play I would have identified it as a *key speech*.

I shall now summarise the whole process from the moment of reading the question before adding a few extra words of advice. You must proceed step-by-step as follows.

1 *Read the question carefully, underlining important words and phrases*
2 *Form a number of questions out of these key words*
3 *Decide what statements you want to make about the play in relation to the questions*
4 *Select the examples you will use as evidence to back up your statements*
5 *Decide on a logical order for the statements and thus for your paragraphs*
6 *Write a simple opening paragraph which briefly outlines your intentions for the essay*

7   *Present your argument in uncluttered language and structured in
    paragraphs. Each paragraph should be clearly structured, move to a
    conclusion, and link to the next paragraph, with the last paragraph
    briefly and clearly summarising the conclusions of your essay*

You may remember that I said earlier that there are various
kinds of question which occur in exams and I have given you
some examples. You may wish to supplement this by looking at
examples of questions set on your particular play from past
papers. This isn't a bad idea in itself but it does highlight the
whole question of *relevance*. If I am asked a question about
verbal communication in *Waiting for Godot* it's no earthly good
my writing about visual symbolism because I happen to have
revised that topic specially in the hope that it would come up.
Nor is it any good my thinking, 'Ah, this is really the same
question as the one they set last year', and reeling off my
carefully prepared answer. You must *read* and *answer* the
question in front of you – no two questions are *ever* the same,
and you must be prepared to apply your understanding of the
play in any way required of you.

To conclude, I shall now turn my attention to the kind of
question which involves reading an extract from a play you
have studied and commenting on it. Your main task is to *identify
precisely what is being asked of you* in relation to the extract. As we
have seen, a dramatic text yields up many kinds of information,
and if you write down everything that occurs to you, you are
going to end up with an excessively long answer which is a
hotch-potch of ideas. On the other hand you should now realise
that the words, the stage directions, the action and the activities
are all equal partners in creating a stage image, so you must use
your practised eye in reading the text. The secret of answering
such questions well is to keep the precise question in mind as
you confront the extract, and gradually to narrow down the
attention you give to both, as follows

1   Read the question through carefully, but don't linger over
    it. Just get a clear sense of what it is asking you to do.
2   Read through the extract fairly quickly and try to establish
    its context in the play. Pause for a few moments to think
    where it fits into the action of the play and imagine the
    action happening in front of you. You ought to be able to

pick up the importance of the particular event selected at this stage.

3 Go back to the question and analyse it. Treat it as we did before and especially underline the key words and phrases which tell you what you are looking for. Two examples might help you here:

Consider the differences of attitude portrayed in the following passage and their effect on the course of action of the play.

(Question on John Arden's *Sergeant Musgrave's Dance*)

Examine the attitudes expressed by the four speeches in the extract printed below, and refer where appropriate to other parts of the play that have influenced your views of these characters.

(Question on Miller's *Death of a Salesman*)

You will see that these are both questions about *attitudes*, and what you are asked to do is to examine how they are revealed in the extract and relate this to the rest of the play. After analysing the question you are ready to proceed to the next step.

4 Comb the extract for evidence of the issue you are discussing. Take your time over this.

5 Think how this evidence relates to the rest of the play.

6 Structure your answer as a brief essay arranged in a series of paragraphs of roughly the same length. Plan your answer in this way and you will avoid giving the impression that you are just jotting down all you know. Instead, try to construct a sensible, logical analysis of the extract.

All the rules for clear, logical writing apply here too and you must demonstrate that you are able to draw from the passage in question all the evidence needed to justify the points you make. Every part of the process of learning I have commended to you in this book will be relevant to this task. But what will also be relevant, and what I hope you have gained from this book, is a keen sense of and interest in modern drama as playtexts.

Further reading

I<small>T</small> is important to use good, accurate editions of your set plays, and the editions published by Methuen, Faber and Faber, and Penguin are invariably reliable. Many such editions have helpful introductory notes; rather more extensive notes and commentary are provided in the *Methuen Student Editions* and the *Hereford Plays* series from Heinemann. Any comments by the playwright are particularly useful, but, like editors' notes, these should only be used to extend your interest in the play, *not* as a substitute for personal engagement with the text. You do need to be aware of 'acting editions' of plays, usually published by Samuel French. These are primarily intended as working playscripts for amateurs and contain suggested set designs and moves which are *not* the work of the playwright. Such additions, though very helpful for amateur companies, were added after the first professional opening of the play and simply give a director's interpretation of the text. These editions are *not* suitable for study purposes.

Once you have become familiar with your set play it can prove useful to read other plays by the same author or from the same period. Very often theatres have suitable texts for sale after performances and there has been a tremendous upsurge recently of publishers such as Pluto Press and Methuen who are willing to put contemporary plays into print quickly and relatively cheaply, so be prepared to visit theatre bookshops.

Once you have studied a play you will certainly find it useful to read something about the playwright and his or her work, as this will enable you to set the play you have studied in a wider context and may give you insights into the issues with which the playwright deals. There are a number of series of inexpensive books giving a critical account of the work of individual playwrights: of these the *Modern Theatre Profile* series (Eyre Methuen) and the *Modern Dramatists* series (Macmillan) contain very readable volumes on all the major modern playwrights, while the *Contemporary Playwrights* series

(Heinemann) deals with all the important dramatists living today.

There are a number of outstanding evaluations of the work of individual playwrights which you should refer to once you have studied your play(s) and, perhaps, read a more general introduction of the kind I have just listed. Examples of this second type of book are Martin Esslin's *Mediations: Essays on Brecht, Beckett and the Media* (Eyre Methuen), or the same author's *The Peopled Wound: A Study of Pinter's Plays*. Finding out about this sort of specialist study is not difficult because they are listed in the bibliography section of those books of a more general nature dealing with the work of individual dramatists or providing a survey of modern drama.

Understanding how your particular play and playwright fit into the pattern of modern drama or what artistic and social forces helped to shape a particular dramatist's response can often be aided by reading a good survey of modern drama or of a particular movement within it. It's always a good idea to read more than one book on the subject so that you get a more balanced view, but very good starting-points would be Raymond Williams' *Drama from Ibsen to Eliot* (Chatto and Windus), John Russell Taylor's *Anger and After* (Penguin) and his *The Rise and Fall of the Well-Made Play* (Methuen), Bamber Gascoigne's *Twentieth Century Drama* (Hutchinson), or Martin Esslin's *The Theatre of the Absurd* (Penguin). You will see that in this brief list there are really two kinds of book. One takes an historical period, while the other examines a particular form or movement. You can usefully supplement the first kind by reading books and articles on the history of the theatre, and you will find particularly detailed advice on how to do this and how to study drama in other ways in *Studying Drama* by David Bradby, Philip Thomas and Kenneth Pickering (Croom Helm). Concepts such as 'the absurd' or 'tragedy', which are fundamental to an understanding of modern drama, are the basis of the second kind of book I have mentioned above. Once you have identified your play as belonging to a recognisable type or category you will want to read more about that issue and you will probably find a relevant volume in the *Critical Idiom* series (Methuen), which deals with such ideas as 'naturalism', 'expressionism' and 'realism' in depth. You will also find very helpful sections on all the terminology we use to discuss modern drama in *Literary Terms and Criticism* by John Peck and Martin Coyle (Macmillan).

So far I have suggested that you read books of criticism to help you form your own response to the plays in question. However, one danger of this can be that you are often exposed to the views of a single writer. As an antidote it is a good idea to read some collections of essays such as contained in *Eliot in Perspective: a Symposium*, edited by Graham Martin (Macmillan), or in the excellent *Casebook* series (Macmillan). These will help you to form a more balanced opinion and will demonstrate to you that experts often disagree. This can seem rather unnerving at first, but in fact it should give you confidence to realise that *your* opinion is as valid as anyone else's provided you form it on the basis of careful study and analysis.

Throughout this book I have urged you to remember that a play is something which takes place in a theatre, and so, in order to understand modern drama, you have to know something about the modern stage. Two of the most stimulating books on the modern theatre are Peter Brook's *The Empty Space* (Penguin) and Charles Marowitz's *The Act of Being* (Secker and Warburg), both of which have influenced the activities I have suggested in parts of this book. You may also find it fascinating to read about some of the great directors who have helped to shape the modern theatre, and you will find excellent books on Brecht, Piscator, Reinhardt and others. All the great directors of the modern period are introduced in *The Director and the Stage* by Edward Braun (Eyre Methuen) and every aspect of the modern theatre is covered in a most useful reference book by Philip Barnes: *A Companion to Post-War British Theatre* (Croom Helm). Finally, it is worth reminding you again that modern drama is a living art and that performances are going on all the time. Records, discussions and reviews of such performances are a valuable addition to your sources of understanding, and you should make a habit of listening to and watching arts programmes on radio and television, and of reading reviews in such magazines as *Plays and Players*, *Drama* and *The Stage* and in daily newspapers, in order to detect reactions to recent productions of modern plays.